RESEARCHING EDUCATIONAL LEADERSHIP AND MANAGEMENT

RESEARCHING EDUCATIONAL LEADERSHIP AND MANAGEMENT

METHODS AND APPROACHES

MARK BRUNDRETT AND CHRISTOPHER RHODES

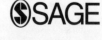

Los Angeles | London | New Delhi
Singapore | Washington DC

Los Angeles | London | New Delhi
Singapore | Washington DC

SAGE Publications Ltd
1 Oliver's Yard
55 City Road
London EC1Y 1SP

SAGE Publications Inc.
2455 Teller Road
Thousand Oaks, California 91320

SAGE Publications India Pvt Ltd
B 1/I 1 Mohan Cooperative Industrial Area
Mathura Road
New Delhi 110 044

SAGE Publications Asia-Pacific Pte Ltd
3 Church Street
#10-04 Samsung Hub
Singapore 049483

Editor: Marianne Lagrange
Assistant editor: Kathryn Bromwich
Editorial Assistant: Rachael Plant
Production editor: Nicola Marshall
Copyeditor: Audrey Scriven
Proofreader: Avril Ehrlich
Indexer: Martin Hargreaves
Marketing manager: Lorna Patkai
Cover design: Lisa Harper
Typeset by: C&M Digitals (P) Ltd, Chennai, India
Printed in India at Replika Press Pvt Ltd

Library of Congress Control Number: 2012949775

British Library Cataloguing in Publication data

A catalogue record for this book is available from
the British Library

ISBN 978-0-85702-830-3
ISBN 978-0-85702-831-0 (pbk)

Contents

List of Tables and Figures

About the Authors

Mark Brundrett taught in secondary, middle and primary schools and was a headteacher for five years before he entered higher education. He has subsequently held posts as Senior Lecturer in Education at Leicester University, Professor of Educational Leadership at the University of Hull, and Senior Research Consultant at the University of Manchester, and he is currently Professor of Educational Research and Head of the Centre for Educational Research and Evaluation at Liverpool John Moores University. He has carried out many research projects specializing in educational leadership and management for individual schools, universities and local and national agencies. He has also written well over 100 published items including many books and articles and he is editor of the journal *Education 3–13*.

Dr Christopher Rhodes worked in schools and colleges for 14 years prior to taking up a post in higher education. He moved to the University of Wolverhampton in 1997 and became Principal Lecturer responsible for leading the postgraduate and professional development studies programme in the School of Education. In 2005 he was appointed to the post of Senior Lecturer in Educational Leadership in the School of Education at the University of Birmingham. His teaching duties include the supervision of PhD and EdD students and he leads the popular EdD programme in Leaders and Leadership in Education. His research activities reflect a long-standing interest in the professional learning of staff and in the development of leaders in particular. Recent works have focused on leadership development and preparation, succession planning and leadership talent management. He is joint editor of the journal *International Studies in Educational Administration* and is married with one daughter.

Preface

This book will outline how interest in research on educational leadership has grown exponentially in recent years. The reasons for this are complex and will be analyzed in some detail, but relate to the notion that education systems and individual educational institutions can be changed for the better if good, well-trained and highly motivated leaders are available to lead change, inspire and encourage colleagues, and put resources to their best use.

In education the vast majority of leaders will be drawn from the 'ranks' of classroom or lecture hall practitioners to take on roles which may require them to lead hundreds or perhaps even thousands of staff. These individuals may also be responsible for organizations whose turnover could range from hundreds of thousands to many millions of pounds, dollars, euros, etc. The journey involved in attaining such leadership posts can often prove challenging and frequently will require further study or training, such as Master's or Doctoral degrees, that will itself include a requirement to gain a strong grasp of research techniques. Once in post such leaders are likely to want to continue to undertake, or at least draw on, research to inform their work or to help in making leadership and management decisions. Equally, there are those who will develop a profound academic interest in leadership research and go on to specialize in the topic as professional researchers or academics, focusing on the study of educational leadership: if this is the case, they will need to become not only proficient but also expert in research techniques. Finally, there are those who are employed by regional and national government agencies, to undertake research that will influence or assess government policies relating to educational leadership strategies: they will need to undertake leadership research either as a specialism or as one element of research on education. This book is intended to be of use to all of these groups and therefore sets out to provide a coherent grounding in basic research techniques that are especially relevant to leadership research.

As its authors we have made the transition from being practitioners in schools to being academics in the field of educational leadership, and since then we have carried out many research studies for local and national agencies. We have also experienced the joys and frustrations of undertaking research for a variety of higher degrees and supervized many students through to the successful completion of undergraduate, Master's and doctoral study. In this process we have gained an understanding of the many challenges that colleagues face in acquiring a real grasp of the research approaches and techniques that will enable a research study to be successful in order to produce the kind of outcomes that can influence and support innovation and change.

Our first chapter explores some of the background to the rise of interest in educational leadership research, explains the nature and structure of the text, and gives some advice on how to make best use of this work. Subsequent chapters go on to examine both quantitative and qualitative approaches to research and attempt to take the reader through the process of preparing to carry out research, designing research tools, and analysing data. The final chapter focuses on the structuring and writing of research reports for various audiences.

We note with some regret that while there is a huge and ever-expanding body of work on educational research methods, there is very little that focuses on the specific issues associated with research on educational leadership. For that reason we have drawn on what material there is in this important sub-field of research, but we have also employed work from the more general field of research methods in education and the wider social sciences. We hope that this book will do something to plug the obvious gap in the literature that must be addressed if educational leaders are to engage in, and with, high quality research. We set out to provide a practical guide to the process of research underpinned by theory, and we remain convinced that leadership research, if carried out systematically and with vigour, confidence, proficiency and skill, can enable our educational leaders to perform better in order to enhance the life chances of pupils and students.

Part 1

Preparing to carry out research on educational leadership

Introduction: Key Issues in Research on Educational Leadership

Aims

Educational leadership (or in previous or alternate incarnations, educational administration and educational management) has been a topic for scholarly activity since the late nineteenth century. However, while interest in this topic has expanded dramatically in recent years there remain comparatively few texts that are devoted to examining how to research leadership practice in educational settings. This book sets out to help anyone wishing to undertake such research to do so systematically and with confidence. Our opening chapter will therefore focus on some of the key issues in relation to research in educational leadership. By the end of it you should be able to:

- understand why educational leadership research has come to the fore in recent years;
- have a firm grasp of the nature of this text;
- understand the importance of gaining a greater knowledge of research approaches by examining the wider literature on research methods;
- perceive the relationships between research, policy and practice;
- know how to use this text to best effect.

The rise of interest in educational leadership

We have already outlined in detail elsewhere how the development of interest in the field of educational leadership arose (see, for instance, Brundrett, 2000), as well as explored some of the key principles in this field (Brundrett, 1999, 2012). In these texts we examined educational administration as a focus for scholarly activity in the late nineteenth century in the USA, when this burgeoning democracy sought new ways to manage an expanding egalitarian system of education. The field subsequently experienced periods where it was influenced by the growing science of business administration (the 1920s) and then the dominant sociological interpretations of education (the 1960s and 1970s), with a more recent focus on school effectiveness and improvement. In recent years there has been a particular emphasis on the development of leadership itself, since this is perceived in many nations to be vital in enhancing the quality of educational institutions and the associated outcomes for pupils and students (Davies and Brundrett, 2010).

We have argued that, crucially, the advent of local management of schools and colleges which took place in the 1980s and 1990s changed the relationship between educational institutions and society to one where schools, colleges and universities became more service orientated, more competitive and effectiveness driven. This presented enormous challenges to the leaders of educational institutions, who had to adapt swiftly to what was a new world of managing staff, budgets, buildings and grounds, as well as maintaining the more traditional focus on teaching and learning (Burton, Brundrett and Jones, 2008). Most leaders took on these roles with alacrity and skill, despite the fact that their initial training would have tended to focus on subject specialism and pedagogy, but some would have found this new environment challenging and irksome: the field no doubt lost some very able school leaders who found the pressures too great. Such losses to a system made up of otherwise capable personnel are sad, especially when they are caused by a paucity of leadership training, or sometimes worse, training that is based on fads or the personal beliefs of individual trainers rather than well-researched facts and approaches.

This new focus on leadership is very much an international phenomenon and a transnational agenda for leadership research, embracing topics such as strategy, learning and teaching, the curriculum, finance and resources, human resource management, and accountability issues. Of course the discourse is nuanced, either subtly or significantly, both by context and culture at the national, regional and local levels (Brundrett and Crawford, 2008). There can also be differences in the foci depending on the phase, although such issues are often more to do with size than with substance since within any one jurisdiction leaders in all phases tend to share the same concerns (Burton and Brundrett, 2005). The ferment in leadership studies that this has caused can sometimes be worryingly akin to the passions aroused by religious fervour, with many commentaries and conferences on leading education encouraging the latest trends, fads and sometimes fantasies that are thought to be efficacious. We would argue that this is in part caused by the fact that educational leadership still lacks rigour in systematic research on what actually works in leading and managing education. This book hopes to contribute to putting right this problematic situation by encouraging sound, focused and well-structured research activity on a topic that is crucially important both to educators and students.

The nature of this book

This book tries to offer a cohesive line of argument constructed by two very experienced practitioners and researchers in the field, and we attempt to offer both a clear presentation of the theoretical underpinnings of research in educational leadership and management and practical advice on research in educational institutions.

We are aware that carrying out leadership research in educational establishments can be extremely rewarding but also often challenging. Because of this we have tried throughout this book to offer a clear conceptual framework for such research, allied with a discussion of the best ways of managing the process of research. In this way, we can offer both a practical guide and a clear grounding and discussion of the underpinning theories associated with research on educational leadership. Overall, our aim has been to both inform and encourage critical reflection through the use of textual features that will prefigure, explore, and then summarize the major learning points relating to research in educational leadership. To do so we explore many, if not most, of the major approaches to both quantitative and qualitative research.

In order to accomplish the goals set out above, the book is carefully structured in such a way that it tries to mirror the journey that a researcher undertakes when engaged in a research project. This includes:

- preparing to undertake research;
- designing and using research tools;
- analyzing data and reporting findings in order to impact on practice.

The three parts follow this structure and each is made up of chapters that are relevant to the aspiring quantitative and qualitative researcher. Part One focuses on preparing to carry out research. Chapters 1 and 2 begin by outlining some of the key issues in the field and exploring some of the main theories of educational research. Chapter 3 provides an initial exploration of the ways in which projects could be designed in order to ensure validity and reliability and trustworthiness in research, and Chapter 4 introduces and explores how a systematic approach to reviewing previous research can help to identify the conceptual and empirical issues that may underpin future research. Centrally, we assert that a researcher should try to define the research issue or overall question or aim as precisely as possible, and in such a way that it cannot be subject to any unintended ambiguity, based on previous research explored in the literature review.

Part Two explores how to design and use a variety of both quantitative and qualitative research tools for leadership research. Chapter 5 focuses on the critically important issue of how to develop a sample that is appropriate for the topic under exploration. Chapter 6 is designed to help readers who may wish to adopt a quantitative approach to leadership research in order to construct high quality questionnaires with appropriate question formats that are suitable for the respondent groups and the conceptual focus of the research. Chapter 7, by contrast, addresses issues connected with the use of interviews, as well as recognizing the strengths and weaknesses of one of the most popular approaches to research in the field. The chapter also offers a great deal of advice on the practicalities of how to construct an interview schedule. Chapter 8 outlines the processes associated with observational research which are so relevant to accountability and school improvement activities and suggests ways to make observation more systematic. Chapter 9 discusses how to gain access to relevant documents and the recording formats that might help in analyzing such material. Chapter 10 focuses on action research, which has become one of the most popular forms of social science research in recent years and is especially relevant to practitioners.

Part Three focuses on analyzing data and reporting findings. Chapter 11 examines ways of analyzing quantitative data, including comparing evidence from different sources, coding, basic statistical methods in analyzing data derived from questionnaires, and online methods of data gathering and analysis. Chapter 12 concentrates on analyzing qualitative data and proposes a four-step approach, including becoming familiar with the data, coding and categorizing, identifying connections between categories, and interpreting the data. Chapter 13 outlines the uses of leadership research and its importance in institutional development, including providing an evidence base for educational improvement strategies, researching leadership for personal and professional development, and enhancing teams. Finally, Chapter 14 concludes the book by discussing how research reports should be written to ensure that key information is collated using an appropriate structure in order to present findings so that they set out recommendations for action.

This overall structure is designed to support our central thesis: that research evidence should be used by policy makers and practitioners at the institutional level to improve the efficacy and impact of leadership, and in such a way that we may enhance the life chances of pupils and students. At the core of this argument is the notion that systematic enquiry, whether it be in the form of qualitative, quantitative or mixed-methods research, should play a major part in achieving desired outcomes.

Developing a greater knowledge of research approaches

In order to further enhance this argument for more systematic enquiry in the field of leadership research in education, we would encourage you to go beyond this text and seek out any other material that may be useful in your developing a greater understanding of research methods. This can be slightly problematic for leadership researchers since there are very few titles that focus on the increasingly important topic of educational leadership research, but the work of Briggs, Coleman and Morrison (2012) is one highly worthwhile text that contains contributions from a wide range of senior academics who outline and analyze the various research methods. However, if you would like to gain a better grasp of the full range of research approaches take a look at the wider literature on research methods. Even if your search is confined to education you will soon become aware that the vast amount of material on the topic is somewhat intimidating, but there are many good general introductions to research methods. These include a general introduction to educational research, also co-written by one of the authors of this text, entitled *Doing Your Research Project* (Burton et al., 2008), which will be referred to throughout this work. The advantage of such material is that it gives new or returning researchers a basic grounding in current perspectives on research and research approaches, and almost all of these add their voice to the central argument of this work: that research needs to be carefully thought through in order to be systematic in its approach, regardless of whichever approach is adopted.

If you are a slightly more advanced researcher, or simply wish to delve more deeply into the topic, it would be helpful if you acquired or at least examined one or more of the more detailed works on research methods. A good starting point would be any of the major standard texts that provide a general overview of research methods (see for example Gall, Gall and Borg, 2006; Cohen, Manion and Morrison, 2007; Newby, 2012). If you wish to expand your horizons a little further and want to examine the overall field of social science research we would recommend you take a look at Bernard (2012) or Bryman (2001). The influential work by Robson (2002) on 'real world research' also remains popular and important, not only for reference but also for directing debate in the field. All of these texts have been highly influential in writing this book, either in the form of direct input or by a more general 'osmosis' of their research approaches and ideas.

We would ask that you remember, however, that even a thorough examination of all of the above would only be scratching the surface of the vast amount of material on the topic. Use of a basic search engine will produce hundreds if not thousands of relevant books and articles which examine, iterate and reiterate the issues associated with research methods both in general and in detail relating to the various paradigms, approaches, tools, techniques, methods of analysis, etc. For this reason we would recommend that you consider carefully which research approach and tools would be appropriate for your work and then explore that material in the appropriate sub-field of case study research, observation technique, statistical research or whatever. Each chapter of this book also includes suggestions for further reading that will help you access additional relevant material on the topic under scrutiny.

Towards research-informed policy and practice

Much has been said in recent years about the need to move towards a system of research-informed policy and practice. No doubt this concept was first encouraged by researchers themselves who had a vested interest in trying to make sure that their work was taken seriously and that funding would continue to be a available. However, there has been a notable emphasis on this same approach by both central and local governments in recent years, and research-informed approaches have been seen as one significant way of improving outcomes across systems. This is to be applauded, but such a concept can also prove problematic since it leaves open some significant questions (What kind of research should be drawn upon? Who should carry out the research? How should such research be funded?). Many governments or government agencies around the world now employ their own researchers in the field of social sciences, and not infrequently these include specialists in educational leadership. Indeed a number of nations have set up or sponsored specialist departments or institutions to conduct research on the topic in order to inform emerging government priorities or changes in the legal framework for schools, colleges and universities. This is generally to be applauded, but if the questions asked and the research agendas set are always defined by governments, then inevitably the nature of the research carried out will tend to focus on whatever political agenda is current. This could then be subject to significant fluctuations as the administration changes or financial and other pressures alter and can mean that original ideas are ignored: the kind of 'blue skies' thinking and research that may eventually lead to truly significant changes in the education system may be given much lower priority when compared to 'quick fixes' that will meet the perceived current need or help address the populist vote winning strategy. This is not to say that university-based or independent research is not without its own problems since, in the obverse, individual researchers or small research centres can often tend to focus on areas of interest that are not necessarily of great relevance to many of those who undertake the day-to-day task of leading and managing educational institutions.

What we are arguing for here is that educational leaders at all levels should take an active interest and lobby for research that is relevant to their own staff and students, as well as take part in national and international debates on leadership research. And in addition to this, we would like to see as many leaders as possible taking part in research themselves and this book is designed to assist in this process. Indeed much of what good leaders do has a close relationship to research, since almost all will be familiar with the process of identifying areas for improvement, auditing current practice, enacting change, monitoring progress, and then seeking to make further developments. This process is derived from the same source as the desire to carry out research and is very closely related to research itself, especially such approaches as action research which follow very much the same structure. What we hope to provide is a deeper understanding of research techniques, based on the accumulated experience of those who have undertaken research on various topics over many years.

Using this book

There is no one right way of using this text and so you may choose to read it as a whole, dip into relevant parts, or use it as an occasional reference point when undertaking research. Since we have attempted to address both the quantitative and qualitative approaches to research, it is inevitable that some chapters will be of greater interest than others depending on your preferred research style and method. For most researchers, this commitment to method will relate to a number of factors such as their own subject background and training, their personal research interests, the topic they wish to research and so on. For instance, it is natural for a specialist in English to want to undertake qualitative research that focuses on the manipulation and analysis of language and text, whilst a trained mathematician would very likely prefer to use a statistical approach since it involves the use of numbers. Such boundaries are not, however, absolute and many will deliberately decide to work outside the range of their previous knowledge. Equally, there has been an increasing acceptance of mixed method or blended approaches to research, and this seems to have been especially the case in leadership research where those involved are often quite pragmatic about which approach they will use, provided it is fit for purpose and leads to the outcomes that they feel are most helpful. If you are in this position it may well be useful to focus on the chapters that relate to the topics with which you are least familiar. However, we would recommend a full reading of the text if you do have sufficient time since in this way you can gain a more complete appreciation of the variety of approaches on offer.

Despite the observation above, that the research approach adopted most often relates to previous experience and qualifications, it is also true that the chosen approach will depend to some extent on a researcher's 'worldview'. By this we mean that some will focus from the outset on finding universal 'truths' that can be generalized to all situations, however small their own particular project. For such researchers the chapters on quantitative methods would, of course, be most helpful. On the other hand, there are some who would reject any notion of objective truth and decide to explore the world of social relationships and the social construction of knowledge. Inevitably such researchers will find the chapters on qualitative methods far more to their taste. Perhaps also there is a third category of researcher who wishes to focus on the improvement of their own practice or the development of the team they manage or the department or institution they lead. In turn, such researchers may find the discussion of action research approaches to be most helpful.

As we have already stated, our aim is to mirror the journey that you as a researcher will undertake when carrying out a research project by offering chapters and sections that focus on research preparation, research design, and analysis and conclusion building. For this reason you might find it useful to re-read sections as you reach a relevant point in your own projects. This is likely to be especially true when points are reached which require a specific understanding of certain technical aspects of the research process (such as methods of data analysis).

The book has also been designed to be especially relevant if you are undertaking small-scale research projects as part of a programme of study, whether for an undergraduate dissertation or for a postgraduate qualification at Master's or Doctoral level, or for a professional qualification. If this is the case a close reading of the entire text may prove helpful, but the sections on research design, the development of tools and methods of analysis may be particularly worthwhile. We would also recommend spending time on the final chapter since this outlines the methods for reporting research findings. These should then help you in producing a sound and readable report if read in conjunction with the specific requirements of the institution or organization managing your qualification.

Summary ☐

This book is designed to meet the needs of those who wish to know more about or to engage in research on educational leadership. It will be of relevance to a variety of audiences regardless of the phase of education or the type of research being conducted. We have structured the text in a deliberate manner to allow readers to develop an understanding of the process of research and the way in which such research can be made more systematic in order to achieve outcomes that may influence both policy and practice in the administration of educational institutions.

In recent years leadership has come to be recognized as a key component in the improvement of individual schools, colleges and higher education institutions in countries around the world, and there is a growing understanding of the positive effects of good leadership on education systems as a whole. At the same time there is an ever-greater commitment to policy based on, or at least informed by, sound research. This book will help readers to carry out leadership research for themselves so that they can develop their own institutions in a way that is grounded in conclusions based on evidence. It is also hoped that it will help them to contribute more readily and more confidently to national and international debates on the future of educational policy.

Further reading

Argyrous, G. (1997) *Statistics for Social Research*. London: Macmillan.

Cohen, L. and Holliday, M. (1996) *Practical Statistics for Students*. London: Paul Chapman.

Denzin, N.K. and Lincoln, Y.S. (2005) *The Sage Handbook of Qualitative Research* (3rd edition). Thousand Oaks, CA: Sage.

Flick, U., Von Kardorff, E. and Steinke, I. (2004) *A Companion to Qualitative Research*. London: Sage.

Scott, D. and Morrison, M. (2007) *Key Ideas in Educational Research*. London: Continuum.

2

Theories of Educational Research

Aims

This chapter addresses some of the complex and vexed questions associated with the various theories surrounding educational research, including the purposes of research, methodology and methods, and the relationship between research and evaluation. It is the many and varied approaches to educational research that give rise to this complexity, and as we will show below there are many within the research community who would argue passionately for one particular approach at the expense of others based on claims which are said to encompass the philosophical worldview of the researcher. It is noted that leadership and management research has a close relationship to the wider field of educational effectiveness and improvement, as well as being dominated by a pragmatic commitment to mixed methods that are seen as being fit for purpose in attempting to improve school outcomes. By the end of this chapter you should be able to:

- understand the purposes of research as a whole and educational leadership research specifically;
- have a sound grasp of the relationship between methodology, method and philosophical approach;
- see how different research paradigms influence the development of a framework for research;
- understand the nature of research strategies;
- be aware of the relationship between research and evaluation.

The purposes of research

School-based research is claimed by Joyce (1991) to be one of the five 'doors' to improving practice within schools and systematic enquiry into how educational institutions are led is, or should be, a crucial component in institutional improvement and improved outcomes. Traditionally, such research has been carried out by 'expert' researchers based in higher education institutions, but recent years have revealed an increasing emphasis on the importance of school-based research as part of continuing professional development and we have argued elsewhere that practitioners need to be seen as equal partners with academic researchers in the process of producing evidence to raise standards (Burton and Brundrett, 2005: 21).

Morrison suggests that educational research has a twin focus: attitudinal – 'a distinctive way of thinking about educational phenomena', and action – a systematic means of investigating them (2002: 3). Brown and Dowling make an attempt to distinguish between 'professional educational practice' – the reflective practitioner – and 'educational research practice' (1998:165) which tries to address and understand the deeper issues underlying educational phenomena by asking the question 'why?' and not just raising the more immediate and more practical considerations of 'what?' and 'how?' This suggests that whilst educational research will certainly influence what happens in the classroom, the major force of its impact will be in the long-term policy decisions made within educational institutions.

Methodology, method and philosophical approach

The difference between methodology and methods is one of the most contested and challenging issues in research. In part, this is an abstract discussion that can be frustrating to students and even professional researchers who simply want to begin to find out what is going on in a given situation or institution, but the discussion about methodology is one which can rarely be sidestepped completely. For instance, there is a general expectation that all students submitting for a research degree will carry out a detailed discussion of the methodology that they have employed and offer a cogent defence of their approach. Equally, when professional researchers submit a proposal or bid for research funding there is often a requirement that they will both outline and justify their methodology, as well as state the research tools that they will employ. The basic confusion is usually between:

- *methodology*, namely the broad system or body of practices and procedures that will be employed to investigate a set of phenomena, and
- *methods*, the actual analytical approaches that will be employed in the research process.

Since one governs or overarches the other, it is inevitable that there will be a considerable overlap when discussing the two concepts.

Both the methodology and methods will depend on your philosophical approach to knowledge and to thinking about your research strategy. *Ontology* is a branch of philosophy concerned with the nature of being and is about matters relating to reality and truth. What is the nature of the world? What really exists? What is reality? There are two extreme positions: on one hand, it can be argued that reality and truth are a 'given' and are external to the individual, but on the other it can also be argued that reality and truth are the product of individual perception. *Epistemology* is the philosophical study of the nature, limits, and grounds of knowledge. It is closely related to ontology but refers to knowledge and its construction/production. It is concerned with what distinguishes different kinds of knowledge claims, i.e., with what the criteria are that allow distinctions to be made and how what exists can be known. What knowledge counts and by what evidence? Again there are two extreme positions. On one hand, it can be argued that knowledge is hard, real, and capable of being transmitted in a tangible form, but it can also be argued that it is subjective and based on experience and insight. For obvious reasons scientists will tend to hold the former view while social scientists will often champion the latter.

The researcher's worldview will impact directly on the overall research approach that they will take since if they subscribe to the scientific approach it is inevitable that both their methodology and methods will reflect those beliefs. Alternatively, if they are social constructivists they are far more likely to employ approaches which will try to elicit rich data via qualitative methods that will allow them to interpret the complex social world they are interested in. For these reasons, broadly speaking, the approaches employed in all research will fall into the general categories of objective/positivist (i.e., following the logic of demonstration), or subjective/interpretive (i.e., following the logic of discovery). We can unpack these terms a little further:

- *Positivism* attempts to apply theory to the research context to assess how applicable these are – that is, to compare an often idealised model in theory with reality. This implies that research should focus on the observable and the measurable, whether in absolute terms or via the perceptions of relevant individuals or groups of individuals. This relationship with the evidence base tends to link positivism with quantitative research, where the measurement of variables and concept formation has a central role and the focus of the research is concerned with the nature of causality.
- *Interpretivism* is a more 'people-centred' approach which acknowledges the research's integration within the research environment – that is, where each will impact on the perceptions and understandings of the other. Interpretivists will immerse themselves in the research environment and attempt to 'explore the "meanings" of events and phenomena from the subjects' perspectives' (Morrison, 2002:18). The evidence collected by interpretivists will be qualitative in nature, offering a rich and deep description of the research environment as a unique context.

While positivism will impose a direction and focus on the research, interpretivism will be driven by the subject, thus adopting a much more holistic and longitudinal perspective. Comparability is of no particular concern to interpretivists as the research becomes the unique 'storyteller' where the story has no

Table 2.1   Opposing research methodologies

Interpretive		Positivist
Reality is a construct. It is multi-dimensional, ever changing, and dependent on different frames of reference.	1. How is reality defined? *(Ontology)*	Reality is to be discovered. It is objective, rational, and independent from the observer.
The research process is underpinned by democratic principles, giving equal status to participants and welcoming a diversity of perspectives. The researcher forms part of the research setting and affects and is affected by it (e.g. insider/outsider position). Issues related to status, power, ownership and control (gender, race, class, culture, political perspective) are important.	2. How does the researcher perceive him/herself in relation to the research setting? *(Positionality)*	The researcher is objective and independent from the research setting/experiment (outsider position). The individual self is suppressed or negated since personal values impair scientific objectivity and impartiality. The researcher operates within clearly defined parameters, following pre-determined procedures. Observation should be uncontaminated by extraneous data.
Qualitative data, but not exclusively. Insights, deeper knowledge and understanding of human behaviour and relationships. Exploring different perspectives relating to one phenomenon. Uniqueness.	3. What is (are) the purpose/aim(s) of the research? *(Rationale)*	Qualitative data. Generalizations. Proving/disproving the hypothesis. Searching for the 'truth'. Hypotheses are derived from theories and are submitted to empirical tests for verification and rejection.
The construction of knowledge is a democratic process, involving both researcher and research participants. Knowledge is constructed from multiple perspectives. The element of subjectivity and bias is acknowledged and declared – the 'belief' system underpinning the viewpoint of the research (e.g. Feminist research).	4. How is knowledge created? *(Epistemology)*	The researcher is perceived as the 'guardian' and 'creator of knowledge' and as such occupies a position of authority in relation to the research 'subjects'. Only those phenomena that are observable and measurable can validly be warranted as knowledge (empiricism).
Theory-building is perceived as an ever-developing entity, not a perfect product. It is central to the research process and emerges from the dialogue	5. What role does theory play?	Theory and hypothesis testing provide the rationale for the research and inform its design. The conceptual framework underpinning the research

(Continued)

Table 2.1 (Continued)

between theoretical and professional perspectives and the data gathered (e.g. Grounded Theory). The conceptual framework around which the research is constructed emerges gradually (inductive method).		design is pre-determined (deductive method).
Credibility and trustworthiness (building confidence in the accuracy of the data). Internal validity (thick description, rich, dense data through triangulation). Transferability, relatability, and translatability of findings across similar settings.	6. What are the quality criteria of 'good' research?	External validity (the data are accurate and also valid in relation to other contexts). Reliability (concerned with the consistency of measure). Generalizability (the research results also apply to other settings). Statistical significance.
Voluntary participation based on informed consent. Anonymity of participants and confidentiality of information divulged. Protection of research participants against potentially harmful consequences. Protection of privacy. Giving voice and ownership to the research participants.	7. What ethical issues need to be considered?	Voluntary participation based on informed consent. Anonymity of participants and confidentiality of information divulged. Protection of research participants against harmful consequences (risk assessment).

(Adapted from Burton et al., 2010: 61–62)

discernible or definitive conclusion: for the positivist, however, comparability is all important. (Table 2.1 outlines the two extremes of what can be seen as competing research paradigms.)

Clearly, these two different approaches are both applicable to educational leadership, with the purposes to which the outcomes of the research are to be put being the main determinant. However, it might be more appropriate to 'mix and match' research strategies, methodologies and methods to meet the needs of the topic. Furthermore, it is probably true to say that most researchers engaged in work on educational leadership and management issues would use either surveys, interviews or a mixture of the two as their preferred method of collecting data and case studies as their methodological approach. Note also that many interview-based surveys will focus on the lives and careers of leaders and so could also be classified as using a biographical methodology. However ethnography in its fullest sense, which 'aims to ascertain the understanding that leaders (and their followers) have of leadership and the factors that shape that understanding' (Gronn and Ribbins, 1996: 458), is little used because of the emphasis placed on direct and systematic observation, which is a very time-consuming activity that requires frequent and sustained access to the sometimes esoteric and ethically problematic world of schools and because ethnographic researchers will need to immerse themselves in the life of an organization and use multiple methods for gathering data.

Paradigms and the development of a framework for research

A further layer of complexity is added when researchers seek to address which paradigm they will adopt. Briggs et al. (2012: 16) argue that this process is based on how researchers make sense of information and transform it into research data by drawing on their epistemological assumptions. In this sense a paradigm is the set of beliefs which a researcher will employ in order to understand the evidence they have obtained: this will then influence their approach to the research. Bryman offers a clear definition here when he observes that a paradigm is:

> ... a cluster of beliefs and dictates which for a scientist in a particular discipline influence what should be studied how research should be done, and how results should be interpreted. (2004: 453)

Scott and Morrison (2006: 170) suggest that a range of paradigms have been developed in the field of educational research and they discuss four of these in some detail:

- *Positivism*, where it is suggested that facts can be collected and collated to either confirm or reject a theory or hypothesis conclusively.
- *Phenomenology*, which places a strong emphasis on interpreting the meaning of phenomena and focuses on human action and its interpretation.
- *Critical theory*, which focuses on values and accepts that the researcher can never be a neutral 'scientific' observer since their very presence changes the phenomena or situation being observed.
- *Postmodernism*, which is a further rejection of the scientific approach with its attempt at universal generalizations, argues instead that there can never be one universal truth since all data are interpreted differently by different observers.

We may recognize, however, that there is significant overlap between all such paradigms apart from the 'hard-line' positivist approach which deals only with verifiable empirical data that will result in universal conclusions. In the end, the most important thing for leadership research in practice is to place that research in some kind of wider framework, and it is the issue of the type of knowledge that researchers are seeking that may relate most closely to the kind of project they choose to undertake. For instance, a researcher might profitably ask whether they are concerned with:

- *instrumentalism*, which tries to disseminate a knowledge of practice and associated skills through training and consultancy from a positive stand-point within the prevailing ideology;
- *reflexive action*, which attempts to develop and share practitioners' own practice knowledge through a self-critical analysis of their work in order to improve their practice, either within the prevailing ideology or according to an alternative ideology;
- *conceptual research*, which challenges and extends knowledge, or;
- *evaluative research*, which seeks to measure the impact of an approach or series of actions (see also Wallace and Poulson, 2003).

A researcher's consideration of which framework fits with the research is critical, not only because it will help them to reflect on which paradigm they fit within but also because it will help them in very practical ways in terms of determining the kinds of question they will ask. Therefore, an instrumentalist researcher will ask which strategies and tactics are being employed by leaders in a school or other educational establishment, but an evaluative researcher will be concerned with questions such as how the impact of leadership in the school is measured. Once again of course you will note that these two approaches are not mutually exclusive in the sense that a researcher would need to examine and evaluate leadership approaches, since there is no point in disseminating leadership practice when its efficacy in improving the work environment, student outcomes and so on has not been examined. There are, however, some in the research community who would look upon evaluation as a type of second-order research which does not have the status of more fundamental approaches to knowledge discovery or examination, but it is often the case that leadership researchers are especially interested in evalua-tion since they are seeking to examine their own or others' practice in order to improve the education system. For this reason, we will focus on evaluation in more detail later in the chapter.

Research strategy

Overall, the main point we must emphasize here is that your philosophical approach will determine your preferred research strategy. For example, the phenomenological strategy described by Denscombe (2003) focuses much more on people's interpretations of events, hence giving rise to *multiple reali-ties* that may be shared by groups of people. In contrast, Trochim's (2002) post-positivist strategy (which by the way rejects the central tenets of positiv-ism) argues that 'the goal of social science is to hold steadfastly to the goal of getting it right about reality, even though we can never achieve that goal' (in other words, arguing for a single but provisional *shared reality* that most people will subscribe to).

Borg and Gall (1989), two of the best known writers on educational research over the last generation, place themselves firmly in the scientific, positivist tradition of educational research by citing the 'chain of reasoning' approach outlined by Krathwohl (1985). Here the research design is conceptualized as a series of links in a chain, each of which must be perfect in order to guarantee the integrity of the overall research design. Using this approach Borg and Gall posit that the test of a knowledge claim has two parts: first, to test whether the knowledge claim is true of the particular situation which the researcher has chosen to observe, and second, to test whether the knowledge claim is likely to hold true in other situations (Borg and Gall, 1989: 325). For them the definition of a research design is thus: 'a process of creating an empirical test to support or refute a knowledge claim' (ibid.: 324). They also go on to suggest nine steps in the production of a robust research approach:

1. Conclusions from previous study.
2. Explanation, rationale, theory, or point of view.
3. Questions, hypotheses, predictions, models.
4. Design of the study.
5. Gathering the data.
6. Summarizing the data.
7. Determining the statistical significance of the results.
8. Conclusions.
9. Beginning of the next study.

This scientific approach to research has many proponents and is often, for obvious reasons, favoured by those with a background in mathematics, the 'hard' sciences and engineering who have both the skills and mindset to be able to carry out such methods. However, there have long been opponents of the positivistic approach in social sciences such as education. Cziko (1989: 17), for example, argued that 'the phenomena studied in the social and behavioural sciences are essentially unpredictable and indeterminate', thus leading to a rejection of ever finding universal laws, a belief that led Cziko to the conclusion that educational research should limit itself to 'describe, appreciate, interpret, and explain social and individual behaviour' (ibid.: 23). Nearly a decade later, Thomas also offered a swinging attack on positivism in educational enquiry, arguing that it is 'formulaic' and 'follows a predictable rut and often leads to uninteresting findings' (1998: 141). This led Thomas to argue for a shift away from a research tradition driven by a desire to 'know what' towards one which would embrace the desire to 'know how' since, he suggested, 'methods of educational research are no more than the technology of consolidation – the cogs and axles of a description of the existing world' and that their use 'merely reinforces the consensual paradigm' (ibid.:153). It is interesting to note that this shift from the 'know how' to the 'know what' approaches seems to mirror the changing balance between school effectiveness and improvement research that took place in the 1980s and 1990s, where the focus gradually moved away from attempts to prove that different approaches to school management could make a difference in outcomes which were dominated by statistical methods, and concentrated on the analysis and exemplification of the actual ways in which schools could operate differently in order to produce those improved outcomes which often employed qualitative methods.

It is unlikely that such 'paradigm wars' will ever reach the point of establishing a firm and lasting peace, but social science researchers have gradually come to accept a 'logic in use' approach which has had its proponents since the 1960s (Kaplan, 1964) and which suggests a 'legitimate complementarity of paradigms' (Salomon, 1991: 10). Such mixed-method or blended approaches have a particular appeal for those who are engaged in educational leadership research who often possess a pragmatic mindset since it is usually true that they would wish to gather both rich case study evidence whilst at the same time making more generalizable findings about leadership across a system of education. These blended approaches have gained further credibility by appearing to lend themselves to recent school effectiveness research especially well (Creemers, Kyriakides and Sammons, 2010) and there are now a number of major texts that provide guidance on mixed-methods research (see, for instance, Plano Clark and Cresswell, 2008; Teddlie and Tashakkori, 2008; Tashakkori and Teddlie, 2010).

The relationship between research and evaluation

We have already pointed out that evaluation is often a popular approach for those engaged in educational leadership research. This is because evaluation processes enable educational institutions to analyze their strengths and weaknesses in a systematic way which can lead to greater effectiveness and ensure good outcomes in accountability processes such as external inspections. We have also argued elsewhere that if such an evaluation is to be accurate researchers need to measure the stage of development against original aims or targets in order to establish how far the individual or group has progressed (Burton and Brundrett, 2005: 187). Evaluation may take place as a discrete, one-off, activity in the form of an individual piece of research, or it may form continual feedback about progress towards the achievement of long-term strategic targets so that there is a learning, feedback and evaluation loop that informs learning and teaching. One of the greatest supporters of school self-evaluation research is MacBeath (1999) who argues that the purposes of evaluation may be varied and might encompass:

organizational development;

improved teaching;

improved learning;

political reasons;

accountability reasons;

professional development reasons.

All of the above issues are undoubtedly central to the enterprise of education, and in an era when accountability processes are increasingly pervasive across many education systems it is of little surprise that much leadership research, whether for in-school purposes, for personal professional development, or for academic or nationally-funded research projects, focuses on such issues. Nonetheless, as we have indicated earlier, evaluation is a contested concept which may appear to be neutral but in practice can be used in many different ways, some of which will challenge our conceptions about our own professionalism and the quality of the teaching that occurs within a school, FE or HE institution (Coleman, 2005: 153). For this reason evaluation may appear to be an objective process, but in fact it can be value laden and reveal many insights about an organization or individuals which may be challenging, controversial, and even dangerous to the organization involved. For instance, evaluation may reveal inadequacies in administration or teaching that can be traced to individuals who may, ultimately, be subject to capability or competence procedures, thus making the process appear threatening and hostile to those members of staff with whom a leader must work.

Equally, we need to be aware that some things are much easier to evaluate than others, which means that we tend to evaluate items that are susceptible to quantifiable analysis (such as examination or assessment successes) or the effects on outcomes associated with curriculum innovations. This is partly because anything that produces quantifiable outcomes has an appeal to the evaluator in that it can be analyzed with clarity, often using simple mathematical models (Burton and Brundrett, 2005: 188). However, we must also remember that there are many things that cannot easily be measured in a quantifiable way such as developments in socialization skills, and improvements in behaviour, attitude and motivation.

Perhaps it is for the reasons outlined above that some members of the research community would tend to avoid evaluative research altogether, or would at least view it as less significant or meritorious than other types of research which attempt to produce new knowledge. This has meant that evaluation has often been a neglected area in research methods in the UK, but the notion of research-informed practitioners and the increasing focus on educational improvement have meant that the topic cannot be ignored and we must seek more rigorous approaches to this important issue. Thus, despite these caveats, it is generally accepted that evaluation is a form of *applied* research (Coleman, 2005: 156). Indeed, Walliman (2005) argues that evaluation should be considered a distinct research approach with two strands:

- *Systems analysis*, which focuses on a holistic approach being taken to the examination of a complex situation (such as classroom or organizational dynamics), which is progressively deconstructed into manageable elements.
- *Responsive evaluation*, which focuses on the analysis of the impact of specific initiatives (such as an innovation in the curriculum or a new leadership structure).

In this way evaluation falls within the positivist paradigm, although some forms of evaluation may justifiably employ qualitative approaches such as interviews or even ethnography within a case study in order to gather rich data on a complex topic (Burton, Brundrett and Jones, 2010: 68). MacBeath et al. (2000) take what is in some ways a simpler view and characterize most evaluation methods as 'asking', which can be accomplished through:

- interviews;
- questionnaires;
- log or diary writing;
- observation and work shadowing;
- focus group discussions.

Evaluation therefore crosses the boundaries between quantitative and qualitative methods, and the main guiding principles on the methods employed should be ease of use and fitness for purpose.

Summary ☐

The overlapping terms 'methodology' and 'paradigm' can often cause confusion for researchers, but it remains the case that there are those in the academic community who would still take a fundamentalist view and insist that only one approach to research is capable of offering appropriate ways of analyzing educational institutions. For positivists the security offered by an objective viewpoint based on the scientific and experimental method is the only way to gain an objective analysis of phenomena. For interpretivists such objectivity is impossible, since the social world of education is incapable of the reduction required by the scientific approach and the rich data that can be gained from qualitative approaches are the only way to provide access to the complexities of educational life. However, it is probably true to say that most of those engaged in leadership research would take a pragmatic view of research, and are prepared to mix and match approaches in order to utilize what they would see as a robust research approach which will be fit for purpose. Indeed, leaders are often most concerned with finding out what does and does not work, and this requires them to focus on applied research in the form of evaluation studies which may generally fall within a positivist tradition, but which do not exclude the use of qualitative research tools focused on individual institutions or groups of institutions. This can sometimes result in leadership researchers being criticized for their failure to focus on the development of fundamental knowledge, but leadership researchers must remain firm in their belief that the improvement of outcomes is important in itself.

Further reading

Alvesson, M. and Skoldberg, K. (2000) *Reflexive Methodology: New Vistas for Qualitative Research.* London: Sage.

Crotty, M. (1998) *The Foundations of Social Research.* London: Sage.

Denzin, N.K. and Lincoln, Y. (1998) *The Landscape of Qualitative Research.* Thousand Oaks, CA: Sage.

Frankfort-Nachmias, C. and Nachmias, D. (1996) *Research Methods in Education* (3rd edition). London: Arnold.

Sarantakos, S. (1998) *Social Research.* London: Macmillan.

Useful websites

AERA (American Education Research Association) www.aera.net/

BERA (British Educational Research Association) http://bera.ac.uk

CERUK (Current Educational Research in the UK) www.ceruk.ac.uk/ceruk/

ICSEI (International Congress for School Effectiveness and Improvement) www.edu.icsei/index.html

Ensuring Reliability, Validity and 'Trustworthiness' in Research

Aims

In academic research papers, theses and dissertations, it is commonplace to see evidence of how researchers have gone about ensuring the quality of their work. References to terms such as 'validity', 'reliability', 'trustworthiness', 'piloting' and 'triangulation' are frequently included. These same terms however may be used in criticizing the research of others, and might also indicate that the quality or authenticity of the research has been compromised in some way by the design adopted or the outcomes claimed. Bush (2007) rightly points out the importance of efforts to ensure the authenticity and quality of leadership research in one's own research endeavours, as well as in assessing the quality of work undertaken by other researchers upon whom we rely to advance the knowledge base available within the field. In this chapter we aim to explore validity, reliability, trustworthiness and triangulation within qualitative and quantitative frames of leadership research. Examples will be given to show how researchers have sought to avoid design pitfalls or outcome claims that may have given rise to criticisms of poor quality or authenticity. The chapter also considers issues of quality and authenticity with respect to a broad range of methodologies and methods, and finally suggests some further reading that may be useful when exploring your own design formulation and execution. By the end of this chapter you should be able to:

- understand the link between high-quality research and educational improvement and effectiveness strategies;
- understand the meaning of key terms such as 'validity', 'reliability' and 'trustworthiness';
- grasp the importance of triangulation and piloting in research;
- perceive the relationship between authenticity, quality and methodologies in research methods.

Introduction

The link between high-quality leadership, educational effectiveness and educational improvement has been reflected in many studies (see for example Teddlie and Reynolds, 2000; Hallinger and Snidvongs, 2005), and leaders possessing the necessary talent to make a difference in this way are able to bring about change in a variety of direct and indirect ways within their organizations (Rhodes and Bisschoff, 2012). The scope of leadership research is potentially vast: for example, Southworth (2002: 74) reminds us that 'we cannot know what effective leadership means unless and until we include the stakeholders' perspectives and their construction of leadership'. Bush (2010) suggests that interest in education leadership has never been greater than it is now. Coupled with this is the desire to advance the leadership knowledge base through research activities and many specialist research journals now exist. Leadership research is also high on local, national and international agendas, and confidence in the quality and trustworthiness of this research endeavour and its outcomes is clearly of great importance. It is incumbent upon researchers at all levels to design and execute research which will bear the scrutiny of other researchers and specialists, as well as any potential users within the public domain. We must strive to seek quality and trustworthiness within the context and frame of the research we undertake. Additionally pertinent to a consideration of trustworthiness in research is the issue of avoiding bias in sampling, as people may well ask if a sample was 'truly representative' (Drever, 1995: 37). (This will be dealt with in Chapter 5.)

Validity

Historically, validity has been viewed as the extent to which an adopted research instrument measures what it purports to measure, and by seeking to increase validity the researcher is also seeking to establish the 'truthfulness' and trustworthiness of the research and enhance its credibility. Validity is an issue when working with qualitative data derived from methods such as interviews, and it is also very pertinent to quantitative data derived from experiments and questionnaires. For example, Parlett and Hamilton argue:

> even the most rigorous statistical survey required constant exercise of human judgment – for example, in what questionnaire items to include, in what statistical comparisons will be made and how; and, most of all, in what light the findings are presented and summarised for others ... Finally there is ... one powerful check on the study's validity – arguably the most powerful of all. Does the study present a 'recognisable reality' for those who read it? (1972: 12)

Thomas (2009) makes a distinction between 'internal validity', which pertains to the extent to which research findings accurately and authentically represent the focus of the research, and external validity, which relates to whether the findings are more widely generalizable to other contexts and settings. With respect to external validity, Thomas (2007) has questioned the validity of some cross-cultural research using self-report questionnaires for quantitative research in educational leadership. This author expressed concerns about how the values of the researchers and respondents may influence both the design and outcomes. For example, it may be that the use of understood 'Western' terminology in data collection instruments is conceptualized differently by those from different cultural backgrounds from where the research is taking place. There is the potential that a researcher may interpret the intended meaning of responses differently and hence put the validity of the research at risk. Thomas (2007) is also concerned that any mistakes made in this way may be perpetuated by other researchers who would continue to rely upon a level of validity in previous findings and methods which may be flawed, and hence would carry potential risks for practice, policy, and the ongoing research agenda. Expressing similar concerns about generalizability and the external validity of cross-cultural research, Brock-Utne (1996) argues for the need for secondary research to re-analyze from an Afro-centric perspective many of the accounts previously written by those from 'Western' countries. She also argues for the use of an autobiographical approach to secure data of a higher ecological (contextually informed) validity.

Note that the extent to which research can be considered to be generalizable is a key consideration in external validity. The term 'generalizability' is used to imply that findings can be applied to a much larger set of circumstances, contexts or populations. Bassey (1999) refers to 'fuzzy' generalization in qualitative research to indicate the uncertainty in translating singular findings from a study to other settings and contexts. There are possible issues here and especially for small-scale researchers in leadership studies. For example, if a researcher was to establish in one college that a particular set of circumstances had resulted in greater levels of collaboration within the senior leadership team, it would be dangerous to assume that these circumstances would exactly apply to senior leadership teams in all colleges. Individuals and contexts vary widely and findings in one context may not transfer easily to others. It might be the case that this researcher's findings could be of value to staff at another college who wish to reflect upon their own work and see it in a different light. In this case, it would be more appropriate to say that the work was relatable to another context. However due caution should be exercised in using findings from leadership studies and assuming their transfer to new contexts, cultures, countries or policy backgrounds.

Nevertheless, there is much that can be done to seek to ensure that internal validity is enhanced within a research study. Denscombe (2003: 301) defines validity as follows:

In a broad sense, validity means that the data and the methods are 'right'. In terms of research data, the notion of validity hinges around whether or not the data reflect the truth, reflect reality and cover the crucial matters. In terms of the methods used to obtain data, validity addresses the question, 'Are we measuring suitable indicators of the concept and are we getting accurate results?'. The idea of validity hinges around the extent to which research data and the methods for obtaining the data are deemed to be accurate, honest and on target.

The aim is to increase validity and decrease invalidity, and by doing so increase the quality, credibility and trustworthiness of the research and its outcomes. For Cohen et al. (2003: 105), 'Validity is an important key to effective research. If a piece of research is invalid then it is worthless. Validity is thus a requirement for both qualitative and qualitative/naturalistic research'.

Internal validity may be increased by using mechanisms such as piloting and triangulation (see below), but it may also be compromised in a number of ways. For example, if questionnaires are not completed truthfully by respondents, or researcher bias intervenes in a way that leads interview responses or compromises objectivity in interpreting findings, then internal validity is necessarily reduced. Cohen et al. (2003) list no fewer than 18 different forms of validity, and these authors are at pains to point out that validity may be addressed in numerous different ways depending on the study and the research paradigm engaged. In qualitative research, as has already been mentioned, researcher objectivity and the use of triangulation can be engaged, whereas in quantitative research, for example, good sampling and the right statistical tests could help improve internal validity. Although validity-enhancing practices do not ensure that a research study is therefore completely accurate, objective and without fault, Norris (1997) does advocate that a practical focus on identifying sources of error and bias, and then reducing such error and bias, would potentially be helpful in increasing validity.

In the introduction to this chapter we stated that confidence in the quality and trustworthiness of research endeavours and their outcomes was of great importance. Further to this, and in seeking to consider issues of validity within her research, a former PhD student of one of the authors, Dr Celia Greenway, engaged in a broadly qualitative case-study approach to assessing perceptions of quality in the early year's sector, with semi-structured interviews as her main method. She included the following extract in her thesis (Greenway, 2011:139):

> In qualitative research entire objectivity is difficult to achieve given that the researcher and all that they bring is part of the process, every attempt was made to ensure that through careful listening, questioning and analysis, contradictions which arose were acknowledged and reflected upon. I also piloted my questionnaire and interview questions. The study attempts to achieve validity by using a number of strategies. Since evidence is gathered using a range of methods this assists the reduction of bias. Bassey (1999) discusses the need to consider 'trustworthiness' as a concept in relation

to case study rather than reliability and validity which are more appropriate to survey and experimental research. His model for building in respect for truth includes consideration of a range of issues which apply to the collection of data, centred on the following questions:

Has there been prolonged engagement with data sources?

Has there been persistent observation of emerging issues?

Have raw data been adequately checked with their sources?

(see Bassey, 1999: 75).

Along with attempting to ensure validity, seeking reliability is also put forward by many authors as a key element in assuring quality and credibility in research endeavours and their outcomes. Originating in a scientific research frame, reliability is essentially regarded as a synonym for the consistency and replicability of outcomes over time, over instruments, and over groups of respondents (Cohen et al., 2003).

Reliability

Thomas (2009) sees reliability as a positivist notion acquired by social scientists from scientific researchers, possibly as a means of adding an element of kudos to their work. He therefore questions its place in social science research design. In essence, reliability pertains to the extent to which a research instrument will give the same result on different occasions, and is rooted in a research tradition where high reliability (reproducibility) is sought by using large samples and performing many replicate experiments or tests to demonstrate that the same results will occur again and again, and that therefore the truth or veracity of the finding is more assured. A simple example of this would be, if you mix chemical A and chemical B together you will always get a resultant chemical C, and you will get this result no matter how many times you mix chemicals A and B together, and no matter if you mix them today, tomorrow, or in five years time, and therefore this finding can be upheld as a scientific fact.

In an educational research context, Denscombe (2003: 300) defines reliability as:

A good level of reliability means that the research instrument produces that same data time after time on each occasion that it is used, and that any variation in the results obtained through using the instrument is due entirely to variations in the thing being measured. None of the variation is due to fluctuations caused by the volatile nature of the research instrument itself. So a research instrument such as a particular experiment or questionnaire is said to be 'reliable' if it is consistent and this is generally deemed to be a good thing as far as research is concerned.

Given that reliability is generally understood as pertaining to the reproducibility of findings, then using a questionnaire or interview on a second occasion with the same respondents in the same context and conditions, and finding that the outcomes on this second occasion were the same or very similar to those secured on the first, would indicate a good level of reliability. Indeed, as Bush (2007) points out, the reliability, or otherwise, of tests is often established by asking people to take the test one week and then calling the same people back to take the same test a week later and then comparing the results. When using questionnaires, reliability may be compromised when the questions include scales that may be sensitive to respondents' immediate mood or feelings at the time. Using a questionnaire with simple, closed questions is more likely to result in answers that are more consistent. As with validity, there is no certainty that all the respondents will understand the questions being asked or answer truthfully. When using interviews, reliability may be compromised by the researcher's own objectivity and consistency. Reliability may also be lessened by the researcher prompting and probing in semi-structured interviews as they seek to increase validity, as inevitably the question schedule may vary a little from one respondent to the next. A real tension exists because greater reliability is achieved by reducing validity. Some respondents may seek to answer in ways that are thought to be acceptable or perhaps in order to try and please the interviewer or alternatively to advance a particular agenda of their own. Again, answers in any of these cases may not be wholly truthful and facts can be 'edited' at source. There may also be a researcher effect in recording, analyzing and interpreting data, and especially qualitative data, as individuals are prone to bring with them experiences, opinions and values from their past. It is important that researchers in these circumstances strive to remain as objective as possible at all times. In seeking to increase reliability a researcher is attempting to reduce any errors and biases in the research.

As mentioned earlier in the chapter, the validity of the research may be increased by piloting the research instruments and using triangulation. It is to these two facets of design we now turn our attention.

Triangulation and piloting

Triangulation invokes the idea of approaching data collection from more than a single point of view. For example, in a research project using more than one researcher in data collection would enable a comparison of their findings to occur, and hence the assurance of validity, consistency and credibility could be enhanced or otherwise. Alternatively, using a variety of respondents drawn from a single group (e.g. heads from different schools) or more than one respondent group (e.g. heads, middle leaders and classroom teachers from a single school) in order to gain additional perspectives on a particular issue may be seen as helpful in enhancing validity. And, using more than one occasion to collect data or more than one method of data collection can also be seen as helpful in increasing validity. Triangulation fosters corroboration and elaboration and hence makes a positive contribution to the likely validity of the findings. Bush (2007) suggests that triangulation pertains to the comparison of several sources of evidence to help determine accuracy and credibility, namely, a sort of cross-checking to help increase validity. In summary, 'methodological triangulation' employs more than one method to research a particular issue, and 'respondent triangulation' entails posing the same or very similar questions to more than one group of respondents. For example, in a study into the role of extracurricular activities in active citizenship education, Keser, Akar and Yildirim (2011) reported that qualitative data were collected through multiple data collection tools, including observation field notes, interviews, and document analysis, in order to achieve triangulation and hence increased trustworthiness. In a study set in the United States concerning teachers' reflections on physical education, Jung (2012) reported that to enhance the trustworthiness of the study, multiple data sources and member-checking were utilized. Member-checking entailed taking interview transcripts, making observation notes, and presenting tentative interpretations back to participants to ask about their accuracy and plausibility. Meanwhile, in a study to explore leadership talent identification and leadership development in schools drawn from the Midlands and the north west of England (see Rhodes, Brundrett and Nevill, 2008), a first phase involved focus group work with a sample of heads, middle leaders and classroom teachers in order to gain a variety of perspectives on the issues at hand. All interviewees were asked the same questions:

1. What do you understand by the terms 'leadership' and 'management'?
2. How is leadership talent identified within your school?

In summary, triangulation can be between methods to address a single problem or within a method (e.g. the views of a variety of different respondents).

Thomas (2009) points out that opinions differ with respect to the need for triangulation; however, on balance, it is suggested that the use of triangulation can potentially increase the validity of research endeavours and that this can only be a good thing. Denzin (1970) highlighted some additional understandings of triangulation. For example, although most studies are undertaken at one time, 'time triangulation' is a term used to convey the idea that responses may be obtained from individuals on more than one occasion, say in a longitudinal study where the changes in respondent views may be revealed over a period of time. (A PhD student of one of the authors is investigating any personal and professional impacts upon teachers who have moved into new school buildings, and has sought teachers' views on several occasions over a period of two years to see if their perceptions had evolved or changed during in this time.) 'Space triangulation' is a term used to convey the idea that if a study is undertaken within a single culture or sub-culture it may not be applicable to, or may be viewed differently, in other cultures or sub-cultures. For example, investigations into leadership and the research outcomes obtained may be strongly influenced by the national culture in which they are undertaken, and alternative perceptions could emerge if a particular study was conducted in another culture. Already in this chapter we have cited the work of Brock-Utne (1996) and Thomas (2007) who expressed concerns about the direct transfer of research findings from one national cultural background to another. Undertaking cross-cultural leadership studies is clearly of great importance in our field, and researchers undertaking international comparative leadership studies are doing valuable work in both contextualizing their findings as well as revealing tenets which are valid and of importance transnationally. Returning to the notion that in order to increase the trustworthiness of a research design and the research outcomes obtained, potential respondents need to understand the questions they are being asked either in interviews or via questionnaires, or in some other instrument requiring them to respond as openly and truthfully as possible. You may already be familiar with the idea of piloting a research instrument. This entails asking individuals, who hold the same or very similar characteristics and background to your intended sample, to try the instrument out in advance of the main study and then offer feedback so that the instrument may be improved, and any ambiguous, misleading, unnecessary or unintelligible elements modified or removed. In this way, the validity of the data obtained may be improved.

Critical reflection upon issues pertaining to validity, reliability and triangulation has been expressed well in the PhD thesis of a former student of one of the authors, Dr Adrian Jarvis, who studied the interaction between subject leaders and their staff in a variety of secondary school departments. He opted for a mixed-methods approach that included interviews, questionnaires and observation. We have included the following extract from his thesis (Jarvis, 2011:136):

> The issue of validity is important when working within a qualitative paradigm. Cohen et al. (2003) define validity by stating that it is "a demonstration that a particular instrument in fact measures what it purports to measure" (p. 105). Gorard (2008) puts the question in terms of the "warrant" that should be given to an evidence-based argument: he urges the researcher to ask of any piece of evidence, "what else might this mean?" before jumping to conclusions. Of most relevance to this research is internal validity – the extent to which findings can be justified by the data presented – rather than external validity – how far findings can be generalised to other settings and replicated by repetition of the research. Schofield (1989) makes a case that qualitative research could be seen as generalizable if the cases studies are in some way 'typical' and studies in sufficient numbers for the data to be trustworthy – this is essentially the issue of triangulation which will be discussed later. If validity

is a fundamental of sound research, there is also a need for the data to be reliable. According to Cohen et al. (2003) reliability is "a synonym for consistency and replicability over time" (p. 117). Denscombe (2003) argues that qualitative research, by its nature, is filtered through the personality of the researcher and this can militate against the reliability of the data gathered. Data have to be considered reliable if they are used to reach convincing conclusions – this is a matter of comprehensive coverage and 'best fit' between what are recoded as data and what actually occurs in the 'real world' (Bogdan and Biklen, 1992). The standard of reliability is determined by how that data are collected. This brings in methods of triangulation and how data are interpreted. Denzin (1970) identifies several types of triangulation: data, investigation, theory and methodological. For this research, the two types of most relevance were data and methodological. Data triangulation means gathering data from a variety of contexts and setting in order to ensure comparability and breadth of coverage. Scott (1996) lists a number of procedures which researchers should follow to achieve this. Methodological triangulation can be split into the 'within-method' approach – which means using the same method on different occasions – or the 'across-method' approach, which involves mixing methods within one overall research design. More problematic is the interpretation and analysis of the data collected. Miles and Huberman (1994) advocate looking for, "patterns and processes, commonalities and differences" (p. 9). Scott (1996) reminds us that interviews are generally given by people talking about events which have occurred at some point in the past, and the only guide to the reliability of the data obtained is the interviewee's memory. To some extent, this problem has been dealt with, in this study, through triangulation.

Given that trustworthiness is relevant across all research approaches, the section below reviews a variety of methodologies and methods commonly adopted by the researcher and comments upon related issues pertaining to validity and reliability.

Authenticity, quality and research methodologies and methods

Thomas (2009) reminds us that in interpretive research the researcher is central in interpreting the findings obtained. As already alluded to in this chapter a researcher has a position, and while they will attempt to maintain objectivity they will come with their own values, pre-conceived ideas, experiences and expectations that could, even in some small way, have a bearing on the research and the expression of its outcomes. For example, Thomas rightly comments that the researcher's gender and social class may be influential in how they see the world. In some studies the respondents may be known to researchers and there can also be friendships or differences in power between those doing the research and those being researched. In such cases it will be necessary to declare any such relationships and acknowledge that they may have some bearing on the outcomes obtained. Again, seeking objectivity at all times is essential in undertaking research.

Feldman (2007) argues for the importance of validity and quality in action research. He advocates that validity is a construct that can be used to evaluate the quality of qualitative studies, including action research. Because the outcomes of such research may well have moral and political dimensions and can substantially affect other people, he reminds researchers that it is essential to consider whether the results of their studies are valid. Once again a key point is made here: that if knowledge is to be provided for recipients such as practitioners, learners and policy makers, that knowledge needs to secure and be capable of commanding a high level of trust and belief. Field (2000) offers a discussion about the use of focus groups as a qualitative method in educational studies. Whilst it is acknowledged that there are a number of drawbacks, such as the possibility of one or two people dominating and therefore potentially compromising quality, much to recommend focus groups is identified. In a more recent study, Chioncel et al. (2003) have also begun the important work of considering how the validity and reliability of focus groups need to be addressed. With questionnaires, Munn and Drever (1996) remind us that there is generally no on-the-spot researcher coming between the respondent and the questions, so clarity and a lack of ambiguity are essential features of these. Careful construction and piloting are similarly essential.

As already raised in this chapter, the use of semi-structured and unstructured methods in case study research comes with the inherent possibility of reduced reliability. Bassey (1999) dismissed the terms 'reliability' and 'validity' for case studies, and sought instead to establish the term 'trustworthiness' as an alternative (having adopted it from work by Lincoln and Guba, 1995). This has since found much favour. For qualitative research, Silverman (1993) points to the need for each interviewee (the same would be true for other methods such as questionnaires) to understand the questions in the same way, and that the validity and reliability of interviews can be enhanced by careful piloting. Whilst using highly structured questions for all interviewees would clearly foster reliability, failing to prompt and probe (changing the script a little) such as is the norm in semi-structured interviews may compromise validity by limiting what respondents actually say to the researcher (Cohen et al., 2003). This creates a well-rehearsed dilemma, but it remains the case that increasing validity is crucial to authentic quality research and this must not be overlooked.

Structured observation using a prescribed and fixed observation schedule should aid reliability as it is highly replicable. However, even when using a fixed observation schedule a threat to reliability can accrue as the observer may by chance see and record 'atypical' events that might well be at odds with the 'norm' and may change if the observation was undertaken at a different time. Whilst participant observation potentially scores well for validity in the sense that the observed are being studied in their own 'natural' context, researcher presence at the event being observed may have an effect on validity and reliability as they could cause changes in the behaviour of those being observed. A low profile approach and efforts to not interact with those being observed could help here, but it is likely that those being observed will pay at least some attention to the researcher. Again, a threat to reliability may come from observer bias as the 'human' element within us may be influenced by previous history and modify how we interpret what we see. Once any findings are available, it may be possible to try and verify these with what has been observed as a means to enhance validity and credibility.

Such verification can also be pursued with other approaches. For example, in the case of interview findings Miles and Huberman (1994) describe three 'nodes' pertaining to the analysis of qualitative data (i.e. data reduction, data display, and data verification). Data reduction includes activities such as coding and identifying emergent themes, while data display may involve the creation of items such as text, figures, tables and graphs. Finally, verification may include, for example, a re-examination of field notes as new thoughts emerge, or testing the emergent conclusions with other research data to further establish the plausibility and credibility of the meaning to emerge and ensure that validity is made more secure. In documentary analysis (see Chapter 9) reliability may be open to question because of issues pertaining to text coding. Consistency in understanding the meaning of words, in coding rules and in category rules is required and will help secure greater reliability. A high degree of reproducibility, either by a single coder or by different coders using the same text, will indicate a good level of reliability. Triangulation may also be utilized to increase validity, for example, by using multiple sources of data, methods or researchers.

Summary   ☐

Researchers in educational leadership need to ensure that their research findings are as trustworthy as possible. Taking steps to address trustworthiness helps to ensure that research outcomes are informative and meaningful for the intended recipients. A notable feature of the available research literature is that amongst the many agreements concerning the need to engage validity, reliability and triangulation, and how this should be done, a great deal of disagreement also exists. Notwithstanding this, the present chapter offers a conceptual and practical take for leadership researchers by following a direction that includes the definition of terms, and how key ideas can be used to justify and make certain that trustworthiness in research is being addressed. It applies these ideas across a variety of methodologies and methods commonly used in leadership research. We hope that you will be able to use this chapter, supplementing it with recommended further reading as required, to address trustworthiness in your own research, and also to assess levels of trust-worthiness in the studies undertaken by other researchers that you encounter within the field.

Further Reading

Blaikie, N. (2003) *Analyzing Quantitative Data: From Description to Explanation*. London: Sage.

Cohen, L., Manion, L. and Morrison, K. (2011) *Research Methods in Education* (7th edition). London: Routledge.

Denscombe, M. (2010) *The Good Research Guide* (4th edition). Maidenhead: Open University Press.

King, N. and Horrocks, C. (2010) *Interviews in Qualitative Research*. London: Sage.

Saldana, J.M. (2009) *The Coding Manual for Qualitative Researchers*. London: Sage.

Reviewing Existing Ideas to Develop a Conceptual Framework

Aims

This chapter will discuss some of the key issues in developing the underpinning rationale for any piece of research. It includes an outline for conducting literature searches, and a discussion of the increasingly popular, and linked, research approach embodied in the notion of a systematic study. An argument is also made that all research studies should be more systematic if researchers are to construct a clear conceptual framework that will underpin their work. Specifically, by the end of this chapter, you should be able to:

- understand the importance of conducting a literature review;
- have a clear understanding of the nature of what is meant by a conceptual framework in research;
- appreciate the need to consider the ideas, concepts and strategies suggested by others in the field;
- have a clear grasp of what it is that makes a study systematic in nature;
- understand how to structure a literature review in order to ensure that it is analytical and critical in nature.

The importance of conducting a good literature review

Conducting a well-thought out and academically robust review of previous literature on a topic is one of the most important elements of a successful research study, both in the social sciences and in most academic research, regardless of the methodology that is being employed or the research paradigm under which you are operating. In effect, you will be undertaking the same task as a researcher in the 'hard' sciences such as physics and chemistry, where they must have a firm grasp of existing theory in order to develop a testable hypothesis that will form the basis of the experiment they wish to carry out. As we have already noted, many researchers in the social sciences will adopt an interpretivist approach which rejects scientific rationalism and therefore they will also reject notions of testable hypotheses, but even so, they will undoubtedly wish to know what kind of research studies have been carried out in their chosen area of interest. It is, however, true that researchers will sometimes choose to explore a topic that has not been scrutinized a great deal in the past, and they may find that there is very little material available on that topic which is relevant to their study. However, this is something of a rare event as it is unusual to find a topic that has been completely unexplored. Very few issues emerge that are entirely without antecedents and a determined and thorough review of the literature will almost always reveal at least some material that you can draw on to help you in your work.

The process of conducting literature reviews has been revolutionized by the increasing, and now ubiquitous, use of electronic database searches that enable us to interrogate vast amounts of literature with speed and with ease. But even the best and most user-friendly of databases will pose certain challenges. The very size of the database can often prove problematic since the insertion of a keyword may produce thousands of responses that will place us in no better a position than if we still relied on a manual examination of card indexes and published summaries of research material according to topic. As such we must possess a series of key skills that will ensure any search can be carried out successfully and in a way that will refine the amount of material to a manageable level.

The nature of literature reviews

A literature review is a summary of what has been published on a topic by other researchers; however it needs to go beyond a mere précis and should offer an analytical account of the issues that are of interest: its role therefore is to offer a 'guiding light' for the entire research process (Scott and Morrison, 2007: 141). All forms of publication, including websites, government publications, pamphlets and articles in journals that are not specifically 'academic' in nature, may be used in the process of developing a review, but you will need to place special weight on research-based texts, research monographs, and articles published in peer-reviewed journals where the items have been scrutinized by fellow academics in order to determine their worth prior to appearing in print.

At its simplest, a review of the literature may be little more than a collation of evidence based on a few minutes spent exploring one particular database, or electronic catalogue search, using only one or two key words. Such an approach is perfectly acceptable if your aim is to find some initial material on an issue of interest. For example, this approach would be suitable as background material for an article in a non-refereed journal or as preparation for a lecture or an interview. This process is also important and may indeed be essential in the initial stages of a research study since it can serve a number of key functions, including:

- providing information as to whether the topic is one that has been explored in detail already, or whether there is a paucity of research on the issue, and this can thereby assist in deciding whether or not to pursue that line of enquiry;

- gathering initial material that will form the basis for a further exploration;

- acting as a 'framing exercise' to set up the parameters of a study by discovering the range of literature and the current state of research and thinking on a topic.

(Burton et al., 2008: 30)

You will need to remember, however, that the full literature review that forms a major element of a research study must be far more detailed, and above all more *systematic*, than a comparatively cursory search and summary of the type described above. Indeed there are those who would argue that a literature review should be considered a method in its own right, one that is characterized by a detailed interrogation of the literature on a topic that involves a critical examination of sources from a range of theoretical perspectives related to the definition and methodologies underpinning those sources (Scott and Morrison, 2007: 142).

One of the main issues here is the differentiation between what is meant by a *search* and a what is meant by a *review*, since a search is the process of accessing and retrieving data whereas the review is the product of the analytical process that is undertaken consequent on one or more searches. In order to be successful in this process you would need to structure your approach in order to ensure that you do not consider large amounts of extraneous material that are not germane to the main issue at hand. This process is also crucial because the structure you adopt in the literature review may determine the structure for the rest of the study, since you will need to reflect back on the material in the literature review to compare and contrast previous research findings with your own emerging ideas. The most common ways to define this structure are in relation to the key themes in the main original research aims or questions, and you must always keep in mind your original aims or overall *AIM* (*Author's Intended Message*) as a way of ensuring that your original goals are never lost from sight throughout the process (Birley and Moreland, 1998: 90). Your review must not be just a descriptive list or summary of the material available; it should:

- synthesize;
- analyze and;
- present a clear line of argument.

This last aspect is probably the most difficult to accomplish, especially for the emerging or new researcher, since such argument should never be solely the unsupported views of that individual. Instead it should be a consistent line of argument that is consonant with the researcher's views based on the evidence. In order to ensure this is accomplished you will need to ask a number of key questions, such as:

- What is the specific thesis, problem, or research question that my literature review helps to define?

- What is the scope of my literature review? What types of publications am I using (e.g. journals, books, government documents, popular media)?

- Have I critically analyzed the literature I used? Have I followed through a set of concepts and questions, comparing items to each other in the ways they deal with them? Instead of just listing and summarizing items, have I assessed them, discussing their strengths and weaknesses?

- Have I cited and discussed studies that are contrary to my perspective?

(University of Melbourne, 2007a)

The resultant literature review should be a piece of discursive and analytical writing organized into sections that present a thematic overview or identify trends in relevant theory (Taylor and Proctor, 2007). Overall, your paramount priority will be to ensure that the review not only presents all of the information that has been found, but that it also offers a defensible line of argument that addresses the main point that underpins the questions you are trying to answer. Such an idea may appear fairly obvious but in truth the process is rather more subtle and complex than it might first appear. If you are a quantitative researcher you are likely to commence your research with a very clear set of questions and a hypothesis that will give rise to an equally clear set of issues that you can explore in the literature review. However, if you are a qualitative researcher you are more likely to start your research with a key issue and a series of slightly more open-ended questions that will allow for a much more expansive and slightly less defined set of initial topics to be explored in the literature. Indeed some research approaches, such as grounded theory, are predicated on the fact that the researcher will allow issues to emerge and ideas to develop as the research progresses, which will mean that new themes will need to be explored in the literature. For this reason it is not unreasonable to say that the approach to the literature review is dependant, at least in part, on a researcher's epistemological perspective, since their view of knowledge and their ideas about research approaches will help to define how the literature review is carried out. This issue will be explored in more detail in the succeeding section of this chapter.

Using a literature review to develop a conceptual framework for a research study

The 'line of argument' that you will need to develop from the literature review relates closely to what is often termed the *conceptual framework* for the research, and by this we mean that group of ideas, concepts and theoretical perspectives that will give an overall structure and coherence to your study (Burton et al., 2008: 37). In constructing this framework you will need to compare and contrast different authors' views on an issue, group together the major themes and lines of argument, analyze and critique the methods used by other researchers, state which studies have had the most impact on current research and the work you are carrying out, as well as summarizing what the literature says.

The resulting assessment of previous studies will enable you to explore your area of interest in considerable depth. The ideas, findings and theoretical perspectives that are the result of this process will then allow you to refine and develop the conceptual framework for your research. This will be an iterative process since, as noted earlier, your initial research ideas and aims will serve to define the key themes and parameters in the literature survey, but the literature survey may serve to contradict your previous conceptions: this might then shut off lines of enquiry or open up entirely new areas of concern that will need to be explored. For this reason, the research questions or issues might require some adjustments or even considerable alterations. You will therefore have to judge which new avenues of exploration may be valuable and relevant, but also be aware that there is always a danger that your study of the literature may open up whole new vistas of research that while potentially fascinating may actually lead you away from your initial purposes, or be so broad as to make the study untenable in terms of the time and resources you have available. The best approach to adopt is to keep in mind the key questions or issues that you identified at the start of the study and then be fairly ruthless in ceasing to explore a new or related topic the moment that it becomes clear it is not contributing substantially to the main issues under scrutiny. We would add, however, that this can often be easier said than done, and these are the kind of judgements that often demand the assistance of an experienced individual such as research supervisor, in the case of those undertaking research for a degree, or an experienced team member or colleague, in the case of independent or funded research projects. It is only with experience that more practiced investigators will be able to judge which avenues of enquiry are likely to be helpful and manageable and those which are not.

As noted earlier, such problems are likely to be far less profound for someone adopting a positivist approach to their research since they are more likely

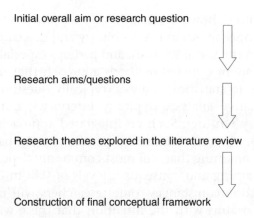

Initial overall aim or research question

Research aims/questions

Research themes explored in the literature review

Construction of final conceptual framework

Figure 4.1   Development of conceptual framework using a positivist approach to research

to see their research as a highly structured process which is characterized by a main question (hypothesis), sub-questions and clear themes to be explored, meaning that a simple schematic such as the one above in Figure 4.1 can be used to represent the process.

By contrast, if you are an interpretivist researcher you are far more likely to follow a more complex route to your final conceptual framework, one that will involve a main aim (an issue to be explored), sub-aims and themes, which may in turn themselves produce new aims and issues in an iterative process which is represented in Figure 4.2.

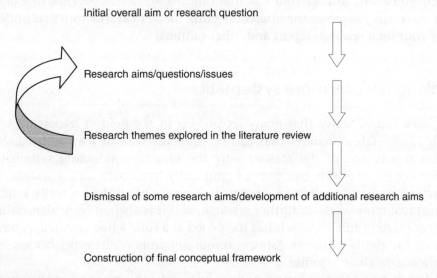

Initial overall aim or research question

Research aims/questions/issues

Research themes explored in the literature review

Dismissal of some research aims/development of additional research aims

Construction of final conceptual framework

Figure 4.2   Development of conceptual framework using an interpretivist approach to research

It should be recognized, however, that this divide between two epistemological perspectives is to some extent itself arbitrary and inaccurate since many of those researching in the social sciences, and perhaps especially in educational leadership, would adopt a mixed-methods approach that involves elements that are susceptible to statistical analysis (typically questionnaires) and may also require qualitative analysis (typically interviews, but sometimes also observation or diary writing). Such an integrated approach means that the aims or questions are more or less fixed depending on the balance of research approaches used, something that will most commonly depend on a researcher's background, training and consequent levels of skill in utilizing different approaches. In such circumstances some researchers will take great care in framing their initial aims with the intention that these will be changed as little as possible in light of the literature review: others will leave the initial aims more general and less concise, with the deliberate intention that the final research aims will emerge as part of the literature review process.

It is probably true to say that most of the researchers who become involved in leadership research will do so because they wish to contribute to better outcomes in the educational institutions in which they work, or at least because they tend to operate using the educational paradigm of school effectiveness which has been dominant in both national and local policy for a number of years. For this reason most researchers in the field will seek to produce outcomes that are generalizable or can be said to offer improvement strategies that will help their institution reach its main goals. This can often result in quite pragmatic decisions being made about research approaches and conceptual framing. Whichever approach you choose to take, the most crucial factor in all of this is that your resultant set of ideas is articulated and defended clearly, so that your research funding agency, supervisor or examiner can easily recognize the interconnecting theoretical structure that underpins your final research report and other outputs.

Making reviews more systematic

We have argued above that many researchers in the field of leadership will wish to generate outcomes that can be generalized or at least utilized. No doubt this is one of the reasons why the idea of conducting systematic reviews of the literature has grown significantly in recent years. A systematic search of previously published studies is one way of creating a really robust conceptual framework for further research, and it is also no coincidence that the adoption of this approach has happened at a time when researchers have gained the ability to interrogate enormous amounts of literature because of electronic database searches.

Whereas a previous generation of researchers had to make do with searching card indexes or other printed material, it is now almost inconceivable that any serious researcher would not wish to interrogate the vast amount of material that is available on the internet or in electronic catalogues or databases. The arrival of the technology to undertake such an approach meant that the critical appraisal and synthesis of research findings in a systematic manner emerged in the 1970s under the term 'meta analysis' – initially in the areas of psychotherapy and medicine. The Evidence for Policy and Practice Information (EPPI) Centre was subsequently established in 1993 to address the need for a systematic approach to the organization and review of evidence-based work on social interventions, and has subsequently become highly influential in the growth of systematic review as an accepted method. The EPPI Centre approach argues that the key features of a systematic review or systematic research synthesis demand that explicit and transparent methods are utilized, that a piece of research following a standard set of stages is used, and that this is accountable, replicable and updateable (EPPI, 2007a). Gough, Oliver and Thomas (2012: 5) suggest that reviewing research systematically involves three key activities:

1. Identifying and describing the relevant literature (mapping the research).

2. Critically appraising the research in a systematic manner.

3. Bringing together the findings into a coherent statement known as a synthesis.

A systematic review is different from a traditional literature review precisely because it attempts to be systematic in its approach. Some of the key ways in which this is achieved are as follows:

- Systematic reviews are *transparent* about how their conclusions are generated. Each piece of research is evaluated and its quality and relevance are made clear.
- A *protocol* sets out how the review is to be conducted before the work starts and is designed to reduce bias.
- *Exhaustive searches* are undertaken to find the relevant research in an effort to discover as much as possible about previous studies which addressed the review's research question. This is a key aspect if the review's conclusions are not to be over-influenced by studies which are simply the easiest to find (usually published research, showing the benefit of interventions).
- A systematic review uses of a set of explicit statements, called *inclusion criteria*, to assess each of the studies found to see if these actually do address a review's research question.
- *Potential users of the review are involved* to make sure that the research is relevant through the use of advisory groups.
- *The findings from sound research are synthesized* to produce clear and easily accessible messages about the reliable evidence that is available on a given topic by appraising individual studies and pooling results.

This last point is one of the most important characteristics of a systematic review, in that it includes a synthesis of its results that is usually presented in the form of a structured narrative, summary tables, or a statistical combination (meta-analysis). This synthesis is then used to formulate conclusions and recommendations (EPPI, 2007b). Some systematic works can be in-depth, with a large degree of analysis of the research field. Syntheses are nearly always in-depth, as detailed scrutiny of the available research is necessary in order to be clear about the trust-worthiness of that research and the relevance and direction of its findings. This time-consuming, but essential, activity means that systematic reviews including a synthesis will often answer a more narrowly focused question. Reviews asking complex questions may be theory-testing reviews using more iterative methods of review, such as in critical interpretive and realist synthesis (EPPI, 2007c).

The structure of a systematic review has been outlined by Gough et al. (2012: 8), who suggested that a clear and coherent pathway should be designed which included the following stages:

- *A review initiation* (forming the review team and engaging stakeholders).
- *A review question and methodology* (formulating the question, the conceptual framework and approach).
- *A search strategy* (searching and screening for inclusion using eligibility criteria).
- *A description of the study characteristics* (the coding to match or build a conceptual framework).
- *A quality and relevance assessment* (applying quality and appraisal criteria).
- *Synthesis* (using the conceptual framework, study codes and quality judgements).
- *The use of reviews* (interpreting and communicating the findings to stakeholders).

The same authors note that two main types of such reviews may be discerned including aggregative reviews, which commonly use quantitative data (where the synthesis is predominantly adding data to answer the review question), and configurative reviews, which commonly use qualitative data (where the synthesis is commonly organizing data from the included studies to answer the review question) (see Gough et al., 2012: 9).

Making literature reviews more systematic

Whether or not you decide to undertake a systematic review rather than a litera-ture review, the development of an orderly and methodical approach to searching for and subsequently examining the literature will be a vital element in the likeli-hood of your research project being successful. For this reason you should strive to make any exploration of the literature as systematic as possible. Figure 4.3

What is the overarching theme of the study?

Define four or five themes derived from research questions/issues/themes.

1.
2.
3.
4.
5.

Brainstorm five keywords for each of the themes to be explored.

1. i.	ii.	iii	iv.	v.
2. i.	ii.	iii.	iv.	v.
3. i.	ii.	iii.	iv.	v.
4. i.	ii.	iii.	iv.	v.
5. i.	ii.	iii.	iv.	v.

Note the electronic databases to be explored.

1.   2.   3.

Outline the key areas to be explored in the review document for each item scrutinized, including:

Full reference with author/s, title, place of publication, edition, page numbers
Source (database)
Methodology employed by authors
Key themes
Key findings
Notes

List the key features that make your approach *systematic*.

Figure 4.3   Systematic Literature Review Toolkit

presents a toolkit for making your literature searches more systematic through a logical process of identifying key issues based on utilizing research aims to inform research themes, leading to a rationale for database searches.

Once you have identified the relevant literature you should adopt a critical approach to reading materials which will help you focus your thoughts. The following points might be helpful here:

- Skim the headings and the abstract of the piece, perhaps looking at the first line of each paragraph and the conclusion.

- Keep a critical focus. Who are the authors of this piece? What do you know about them? Are they leaders in the field or minor commentators?

- Ask yourself what the writer's perspective is (for instance, think about the contexts of gender and culture.)

- Consider if the arguments are logical.

- Establish if there is reliable evidence to support the author's contentions.

(University of Melbourne, 2007b)

The extent to which you follow this critical approach will help to determine the final quality of the written review. Problems in acquiring and storing material have been minimized in recent years since most journals are now produced in a digital form as well as hardcopy, and provided your searches are carried out via an accredited university or other institutional search system, you will be able to download whole articles and documents from publishers' websites. Nonetheless, this mass of material will itself present challenges and you should try to be systematic in the way you store documents. A simple system of creating folders and sub-folders that will reflect the themes in searches, possibly allied to the actual key words entered, will enable their subsequent speedy retrieval as well as obviate the need for much agonizing when trying to locate 'lost' documents.

The systematic review process has as one of its elements the notion that a clear and consistent method of review for each retrieved item should be set up. If you are a lone researcher you may decide to employ a wide range of alternative techniques such as simple note taking, but there is no reason why even the smallest of studies should not employ a simple review document to record the seminal details of the items examined. Figure 4.4 provides an example of this.

Review document
Title:
Authors:
Full reference:
Methodology:
Key themes:
Key findings:
Notes:

Figure 4.4   Literature review/systematic review document

Whether or not you use such a document, try to make some connections between the project aims and the material being read, and compare and contrast the authors' views as the 'narrative' of the research unfolds. In this way you will be able to collate the mass of material on offer and formulate a conceptual map of the topic. It is to this final collation of material into the actual review that we next turn.

Organizing material in a review

Whether you decide to carry out a 'traditional' review of the literature or adopt a more systematic approach, once your searches have been carried out it is vital that you take a structured approach to organizing your material. This is because the use of electronic searches is likely to produce very large amounts of material and it is easy to then become overwhelmed with the sheer volume of books, articles, documents and references you have accumulated.

Working electronically can also help this process along. For example, electronic records of your results can be downloaded from databases and imported into reference management software such as EndNote (see www.endnote.com or Reference Manager at www.refman.com), and more detailed information can be held in a database (constructed by yourself as the researcher or by the research team, or by utilizing a commercial package such as Microsoft Access). Equally, in analysing the results you might want to use systems such as NVivo (www.qsrinternational.com/products_nvivo.aspxand) or NUD*IST (www.qsrinternational.com) (EPPI, 2007d). However, there is still a lot to be said for using some simple approaches to structuring the material you find, especially if the work is on a comparatively small scale where using sophisticated electronic packages may in itself be time consuming and unwieldy. Some basic methods that are often useful are as follow:

- Keep separate files for the different research themes (these can be both physical files for paper-based materials and electronic files for downloaded materials).
- Use a simple method for coding documents that will allow you to discern the material that is of most use to you (such as highlighting the titles of documents that appear to be most relevant, or using a 'star' system to rank each document according to its relevance).
- Structure the material so that some form of logical nomenclature can be applied to it (such as placing items in their date order within themes and sub-themes).
- Above all, do make sure that you keep full references for all these items since it is an all too frequent problem in research to find that a host of material that needs to be included in the final review is lacking all or part of a reference, thus necessitating many hours of further searches to retrieve a name, date, full title and so on.

Your final review must be presented in a clear and structured way. By far the most common way of accomplishing this is to adopt a structure based on the key themes derived from the research questions or issues, and so you will need to be explicit about how studies were singled out for description in a review and methodical when presenting the details of these different studies. Your synthesis will usually need to be presented in the form of a structured narrative and this may include summary tables or a statistical combination (meta-analysis) which can then be used to formulate your conclusions and recommendations. The consequent synthesis should be more than a listing of the results of individual studies and can take a variety of forms. The EPPI method is one which, not surprisingly, suggests a number of highly structured approaches to syntheses, and the most relevant of these for a single researcher undertaking leadership research is probably the *Narrative Empirical Synthesis*: this brings together the results of empirical research in a narrative form to provide an accessible combination of results from individual studies in structured narratives or summary tables (EPPI, 2007e).

Producing this narrative can be a complex and even frustrating business for researchers, whether they are new to the task or highly experienced, since it is common to find that no 'natural' or obvious structure emerges for the material that has been gathered beyond a number of sub-themes. Lambert (2012: 93) suggests adopting a *funnel* approach in setting out a review, starting with the big, wide issues relating to a topic and then gradually working down to the narrow, closely defined issues of the specific topic of the study. This is good advice in terms of beginning to structure the main questions and themes, but it is organizing the material within themes that is often the most problematic and time consuming. If you choose to utilize this approach you will need to undertake a process of *progressive funnelling* so that major themes and sub-themes are identified at different levels within the study. However you will also need to take care that you do not produce a review that consists of multiple layers of themes in diminishing order of importance if the all-important narrative of issues is to be established. Many researchers will be counselled not to place their work in date order in the final synthesis, but in fact this approach can pay dividends since it can be a great help in establishing the interplay and flow of ideas over a given period of time, where the various articles, books and pieces of legislation take up the research of previous writers and amend and develop the body of knowledge and ideas. In this sense a researcher is trying to give an historical overview of the development of ideas and legislation related to their topic. Overall your review might follow the funnelling structure represented below:

- Start with the 'big picture' relating to the topic under scrutiny in terms of the international and national framework in legislation, if any, and the main ideas of the 'key players' on the topic, and then use these to create the main aims and initial conceptual framework.

- Progressively focus on the smaller macro issues, both geographically in terms of the research focus and theoretically in terms of the main sub-themes.
- Initially arrange material in its date order of publication, and then look for minor sub-themes in the major issues which will themselves relate to the research aims.
- Try to create both an historical overview of the development of the topic and a thematic analysis of the ideas and issues.

The key words that are most commonly applied to literature reviews in terms of assessing their quality are the extent to which the review is *analytical* and *critical* and the extent to which it offers a *synthesis* of the material. By this we mean the extent to which the material has been integrated into a clear line of argument which examines previous research studies in such a way that this subjects them to scrutiny in terms of the quality of the research, and the validity of their findings, rather than offering a mere précis of what has gone before.

Summary ☐

In this chapter, we have attempted to outline the ways in which you as a researcher can interrogate previous research in order to develop a conceptual framework for your work, and also make yourself ready to compare your own subsequent research findings with previous work on a topic. We have argued that the systematic review model, which is undoubtedly becoming increasingly influential across the social sciences, is one which you might want to adopt in order to make certain that this process is sufficiently thorough. You may wish to note that in social research one of the purposes of the literature review is to 'pay homage' to those researchers who have gone before and whose work has been influential (Thody, 2006: 91), but the systematic approach will offer some insurance that an analytical and thorough search has to take place, even if the aims do not include a desire to complete a formal met-analysis of previous outputs. Indeed many funding agencies will expect or require a systematic study of the literature as a precursor to subsequent empirical study.

The initial decisions about the ways in which research questions will be framed will relate to the epistemological position of the researcher and, more pragmatically, to the background knowledge and skills that they bring to the research. Such questions or issues are then likely to be the most significant factor in shaping the subsequent structure of the literature review itself. Whether or not you then decide as a researcher to undertake a systematic review in the fullest sense of that term, it would be wise if you try your best to ensure that the interrogation of the literature is as rigorous as possible so that you may gain the most extensive overview you can of the topic you are examining. For many researchers there will then be a subtle interplay with the original aims of the work in order to finalize the conceptual framework for the research and the content of the review. That review should be structured clearly and presented in such a way as to offer both the broad sweep of ideas and a detailed analysis of key thoughts, ideas and past research findings. This not only presents but also analyzes, so the review can truly be said to be an analytical and critical synthesis of what has gone before.

Further reading

Bell, J. (2012) *Doing your Research Project.* Milton Keynes: Open University Press.

Blaxter, L., Hughes, C. and Tight, M. (1996) *How to Research.* Buckingham: Open University Press.

Lambert, M. (2012) *A Beginner's Guide to Doing Your Research Project.* London: Sage.

Orna, E. and Stevens, G. (1995) *Managing Information for Research.* Buckingham: Open University Press.

Potter, S. (ed.) (2002) *Doing Postgraduate Research.* London: Sage.

Thomas, J. and Harden, A. (2003) 'Practical systems for systematic reviews of research to inform policy and practice in education', in L. Anderson and J. Bennett (eds), *Evidence-Informed Policy and Practice in Educational Leadership and Management: Applications and Controversies.* London: Paul Chapman. pp. 39–54.

Part 2

Designing and using research tools for educational leadership research

5

Developing a Sample

Aims

Definitions of educational leadership are numerous and generally centre on a notion of leadership being a social interaction in which followers are engaged in actions to effect the achievement of desirable goals for learners and their communities. In doing so leaders can aid the life trajectories of individuals and local, national, and international interests. The expression of educational leadership is necessarily modified by individual and national cultural and policy influences, but retains at its core a duty to enable teaching and learning to advance and improve to the benefit of the community served. Given the wide responsibility and potential complexity of leadership enactment, it is not surprising that even some years ago Rost (1991: 4) commented that 'many scholars have wondered why we have not been able to get a conceptual handle on the word leadership'. More recently, Bush (2010) has also recognized that the scope of leadership has increased in many countries via a direct devolution of responsibilities to educational organizations. Conceptualizing, describing and theorizing leadership and its enactment in specific contexts, as well as the impact it has on the wide array of stakeholders, will present many challenges and opportunities for leadership researchers and give rise to numerous questions. Who makes up the population of potential informants that are of interest to you as a leadership researcher? Is it all lecturers within a particular college? All teachers within a particular network of schools? And as a researcher, would you be able to access all of these individuals? Would a sample of these individuals be sufficient, and if so who would make up the sample and how would you choose these participants? Would they come from a single institution or from several institutions? And are you intending that the sample selected will be in some way representative of the total potential population or not? In this chapter we aim to explore key items pertaining to access to research sites and individuals, the representativeness of samples and sampling strategy, issues of sample size in both quantitative and qualitative studies and what may be considered as units of analysis in leadership research. By the end of this chapter you should be able to:

- understand the importance of representativeness in the strategy used for sampling;
- recognize the main concepts associated with case study and sampling;
- grasp the importance of sample size and sample composition;
- be familiar with the main issues relating to the unit of analysis in research.

Introduction

Thomas (2009) suggests that a sample pertains to the selection of a manageable group, or groups, which represent the total number of individuals that could have been included in a study. This total number of possible individuals is usually referred to as the population, and the sample represents this population by mirroring its characteristics (perhaps, for example, in terms of gender, experience and context). Whilst some samples are not intended to be wholly representative and this will be explored later in this chapter, Thomas also points out that the intended representativeness of a sample may be compromised by 'selection bias' and this in turn could lead to a possible distortion of the evidence. For example, if you are a leadership researcher who wants to assess the job satisfaction of leaders working in a group of schools located in sub-urban and rural settings, but in the event you only manage to access individuals who are working in small rural primary schools because they are well known to you, it is clear that that sample would not be representative and your overall findings and conclusion may be significantly influenced.

Accessing individuals has its challenges as does accessing research sites themselves, whether they are schools, colleges, universities or some related government office or associated organization. Walford (2001) points out the possible temptation and inherent dangers of simply choosing research sites because they are convenient for research. It may be that such 'convenience sampling', as Cohen et al. (2003) describe it, would be perfectly adequate for the study, but compromising the quality of the research for convenience sake is clearly not a wise move. Walford (2001) suggests that gaining access to a site is often best done incrementally, as the researcher builds trust and becomes increasingly familiar to potential participants. Ball (1990) also points out that the first stage should involve contacting the principal or headteacher, who may allow entry to the site but not necessarily access to members of staff or learners who may be the subject of the intended research. Although it is likely that the endorsement of a senior figure within the organization will have some influence upon the intended participants, ethically it is essential that all research subjects are informed of what their participation will entail, their right to confidentiality and anonymity, and their right to refuse to participate or withdraw if they see fit (BERA, 2011). Note also that gaining access to children as research respondents carries with it its own particular ethical responsibilities and all appropriate permissions must be obtained.

From our own experience, educational organizations and the staff within them are usually very busy, so it will be incumbent on you as a leadership researcher to be clear about what is expected from participants in terms of the subjects you can pursue and the time involved in their acting as research respondents. It always helps if the organization can see some small benefit to themselves in participating. For example, giving them access to any headlines that emerge from a subsequent report or engaging with a new area of thinking they have not considered before can help smooth your access and participation in the face of any time constraints they will inevitably face. Indeed participants, and their organizations, should have our gratitude for the amount of time they so often agree to give to leadership research. With your entry and access secured, you will be able to proceed with sampling having considered the key items of representativeness and your sampling strategy, size and composition, as well as the unit of analysis that is of interest to you in your research project.

Representativeness and sampling strategy

As a researcher if you have access to an entire population, and each individual within it has an equal chance of being selected, then this is termed 'probability sampling'. Within probability sampling a wide range of sampling strategies is available (and have been widely reported: see, for example, Briggs and Coleman, 2007; Thomas, 2009). Some of the strategies commonly used in leadership research are elaborated below.

A random sample *(a probability sample)*
Here individuals composing the sample are selected at random from the population. For this you could use a table of random numbers to do this in a completely random way. Your sample may well be representative of the entire population if you take a large enough group to lessen the possibility of un-representativeness (see sample size below).

A stratified sample *(a probability sample)*
Suppose your research was intended to compare some aspect of leadership between senior leaders and middle leaders: a random sampling strategy of the entire population could by chance result in a preponderance of either senior leaders or middle leaders in that sample. Stratifying could help you increase the representativeness of the sample. In this case, if you divided your population into two groups (senior leaders and middle leaders) then you take a random sample of each group to ensure that your overall sample included sufficient representatives of both types of leaders. Stratifying the sample could help you ensure a greater representativeness of, for example, gender or the type of educational organization respondents taught in, and thus would better reflect the characteristics of your population as a whole.

A cluster sample *(a probability sample)*
Sampling could also occur by dint of your interest in a particular group or cluster. For example, a cluster may be in the form of a network, a particular

school, or a section of a local authority, and individuals within that cluster might be accessible and suitable for random sampling.

However, it could be the case that you are unable or do not want to access and randomly sample every member of a particular school, network, or section of a local authority. In this event you can then utilize other types of sampling. In 'non-probability sampling' you may not have, or may not want, access to an entire population.

A convenience or opportunity sample
(a non-probability sample)
Such sampling secures a sample that is easy to access but will not be representative of an entire population. An exaggerated example would, for convenience sake, include your immediate friends or colleagues in the sample. Note that this type of sampling would also limit any claims for the generalizability of the outcomes of your research (see Chapter 3). Another danger with a convenience or opportunity sample is that you may happen to encounter and include a selection of individuals who, for example, may have a particular grievance with an organization which was not shared by the overwhelming majority of the staff: this would in turn introduce bias into your findings. Nevertheless, and assuming that your sample does not introduce any overt bias, opportunity samples can prove useful, and a broad composition of characteristics may have some value in first studies so that you might begin to understand what the pertinent issues are and what the perceptions of individuals may be.

A purposive sample *(a non-probability sample)*
In this case, you would have to purposefully select individuals to include in the sample because they have importance within your proposed research. They may have particular knowledge or experience, say, and in this way may be typical of the wider population of such individuals. For example, if a study was concerned with the early incumbency of new headteachers in small rural primary schools, then a sample of such heads could be presented as being similar to some extent to other newly-appointed heads in small rural primary schools. Although representativeness is not assured here, this is a common sampling strategy in leadership studies as it does lead researchers to the type of individuals they are interested in researching.

A snowball sample *(a non-probability sample)*
In this type of sample, you will already have secured a core group of individual respondents who will fit your desired criteria and characteristics, but in insufficient numbers to constitute the entire sample you seek. If you have difficulty finding others to join your sample, you could ask the core group to

identify other individuals that they know possess the same or very similar characteristics to themselves. In this way you could perhaps approach them and include them in the sample if they are amenable to this.

The following extract is taken from the PhD thesis of a former student of one of the authors, Dr Adrian Jarvis, who studied the interaction between subject leaders and their staff in a variety of secondary school departments. It shows that a 'random' sample was engaged in an initial questionnaire survey prior to a more purposively selected interview sample:

> The pilot studies, as we have seen, led to a design based on a first stage consisting of the distribution of survey-style questionnaires to respondents in as large a number of schools as possible. In arriving at this determination, it was important as Munn and Drever (1995) point out, to put a great deal of effort into, "defining clearly the group or groups of people that the research is interested in" (p 13). Given the overall research problem and the research questions emanating from it, this was relatively easy to accomplish in broad principle: the population under consideration was that of secondary school subject leaders and members of their departments. This however, begged a number of further questions. Perhaps of greatest significance was that of how representative of all academic departments in all schools did the sample need to be? Given the research questions, the major determinant of an individual's suitability to participate was their membership of an academic department, either as leader or assistant teacher. Therefore, it was not considered necessary to restrict the survey to schools of specific types or from specific sectors. The sample of individual participants chosen, then, can be described as "random" in the sense outlined by Gillham (2000) when he writes that, "in a random sample each individual in a given population has an equal chance of being selected" (p.18). (Jarvis, 2011: 105)

Case study as 'sample'

An examination of the research literature shows us that the use of case studies as the focus for leadership research is commonplace. A case study is generally taken to mean an in-depth study undertaken within a defined boundary of space and time (Bassey, 1999; 2007), pertaining, for example, to an institution (or institutions) and chosen events within that institution that are worthy of study and may be of interest to others, both within the case institution itself and also to a wider field and practitioner audience. A case study within a particular educational organization enables the complexity of real conceptualisations and enactments to be drawn out and outcomes to be communicated to others within the confines of the level of trustworthiness that the researcher achieves within the research (see Chapter 3).

Related to the notion of focus on the actions of individuals in specific circumstances, Cohen et al. (2003) suggest that a case study enables a unique example of real people in real situations that can be clearly understood. Because case study research enables the capture of the different viewpoints of individuals within the particular case studies, Adelman, Kemmis and Jenkins

(1980) suggest that case studies can reflect the 'multiple realities' of real life. Indeed individual cases can have value. For example, Stake (1995) suggests that intrinsic case studies are specifically undertaken to understand a particular question or problem. Instrumental case studies involve the examination of a distinct case and are intended to provide some insight into an issue or theory. Finally, Stake suggests that collective or 'multiple case-studies', consisting of a group of cases, are carried out to provide, as Yin (1989) would advocate, a fuller and more robust picture.

It is notable that in his book concerned with conducting semi-structured interviews, Drever (1995) uses the term 'quota sampling', which is a departure from random sampling driven by the purpose of the research. For example, if the leadership researcher was interested in examining the introduction of a significant innovation to an educational organization (as an example Drever uses the devolution of financial responsibility to the organization), then this change would have different implications for individuals depending on their leadership, management, teaching or support roles within that organization. By sampling these various levels within the organization (namely, a quota of each), a good case study can be achieved. Whilst asking similar questions where possible, it is likely in these circumstances that some variation in the questions used would be most helpful in gaining as rich data as possible from individuals located at different levels within the organization. For these reasons, Drever (1995) differentiates this sampling strategy from a survey approach where all the participants may be asked exactly the same questions.

Sample size and composition

Foy (1998) reminds us that international comparative assessments in education are often controversial, and points out that past studies have often been criticized over the sampling conducted as samples may not be representative or random, and in some the exclusion of low achievers has been held to have biased the results. (The potential difficulties in working with chosen samples and the resultant trustworthiness were explored in Chapter 3 of this book.) For example, in work by Brock-Utne (1996) and Thomas (2007) there was concern expressed at the 'Western' terminology used in data collection instruments, and the subsequent interpretation of those data obtained by researchers with different national cultural backgrounds from those being researched. When you are comparing samples cross-nationally and cross-culturally, it is inevitable that in some cases your findings may be influenced by the prevailing national culture, policy background, and socio-political regime.

In quantitative research projects Denscombe (2003) suggests a minimum sample size of 30 for a survey or exploratory study should the researcher intend to apply an inferential statistical analysis to the data collected. However, do remember that for some non-parametric statistical tests a smaller sample size can be used (see Chapter 11). Whilst many would feel that the larger the sample the more confidence there should be in generalizing from it, this may not always be the case, and large but unrepresentative samples will have omissions that do not mirror the total population (see below). Another factor you may need to consider in quantitative questionnaire surveys is response rates. If only a small number of your intended sample actually returns a completed questionnaire, then you will have to contend with further concerns about un-representativeness as, for example, only a vocal and perhaps biased sub-group may have responded. (Suggestions for maximizing your return rates from questionnaires are given in Chapter 6.) Fogelman and Comber (2007) suggest that given the time pressures that many who work in educational settings now experience, a response rate of 60% for a postal survey is considered to be acceptable. Verma and Mallick (1999) also suggest that an initial response rate of less than 20% would be disappointing. Follow-ups to seek returns or replacement individuals could be utilized here to increase your return rate and therefore the likelihood of a more representative sample. As a researcher you will need to do the best you can in this respect, and it is proper to acknowledge any possible limitations in your work when you write up the research report.

In seeking to arrive at what might be an appropriate sample size for a questionnaire survey, we will give the example of work by a recent EdD (Doctor of Education) student in leaders and leadership education supervised by one of the authors, Dr Alan Kirsz, who set out to establish what adult volunteers in a leadership role knew and understood about leadership. These adult volunteers were from the Scout Association, and the outcomes of the research were intended to enable that organization to reflect upon on its adult leader training programmes. What follows is an extract from his thesis which shows his thinking on sample size with respect to the questionnaire survey used as the main method in this study. It draws upon the notion of confidence levels and sampling error to help determine the size of a random sample (see below). Note that both descriptive and inferential statistics were used to analyze the questionnaire returns (see Chapter 11 of this book):

> The sample size was 400. This was 50% of the total population of 800 leaders holding warrants in the Scout County. Since it is a heterogeneous population a large sample was necessary (Cohen et al., 2000). In addition, Cohen et al. (2000) note that a sample size of 30 is identified by many researchers as a minimum for statistical analysis. They record that for total populations of 500 and 1000 for a sampling error of 5% with a confidence level of 95% the size of samples need to be 217 and 278 respectively. Clearly a sample size of 400 out of 800 meets this criterion and is regarded as representative. It is recognised that this does not take into account the response rate. (Kirsz, 2007: 111)

The quality of your research (see Chapter 3) may be influenced by the sampling strategy you use. How your samples will be achieved needs to be decided on at the design stage of your study. As already intimated, respondent accessibility will also need to be a consideration here. Seeking representativeness in a sample is not necessarily a straightforward task, and the sample and its size will be influenced by the purpose of your research and its nature. A minimum sample size of 30 is generally held (see Denscombe, 2003) as appropriate for quantitative surveys that seek to engage inferential statistics in the subsequent analysis of data collected. Given that you have the time and other resources available to do this in the first place, it is worthwhile to remember that engaging a large quantitative sample will not always ensure representativeness. For example, a sample of 1,000 male headteachers does not represent those individuals in a population of headteachers who are female. Equally, a claim from a very small sample in a qualitative study that the 'overwhelming majority' of headteachers hold some opinion is limited if only five were asked and three did espouse that opinion.

Cohen et al. (2003: 93) suggest that the size of a random (probability) sample can be determined in two ways. The researcher may use their judgement and make sure that the characteristics of the sample reflect those of the total population, or they can use a prescribed mathematical table which shows what the size of random sample should be for a given population. Cohen et al. (2003: 95) provide such a table which indicates for the given population size what the sample size should be to address representativeness within 95% and 99% confidence levels. (For example, the table suggests that for a total population of 100 a sample size of 79 would be appropriate, with a confidence level of 95% and a 5% sampling error, but that it should be 99 at a confidence level of 99% with a 1% sampling error.) The larger the total population, the relatively smaller the appropriate sample size is required to be.

It is generally accepted that the outcomes of qualitative research undertaken in particular settings or contexts are likely to be influenced by the settings or context themselves. However, you will need to remember that the setting and context might also be influential in informing your thinking in quantitative research designs. For example, in some of our work using questionnaires to try and establish school practitioner response about the opportunities for leadership talent identification and development occurring within their own schools, we were conscious that the school context may prove influential in the sorts of perceptions staff held in particular schools. In such a study (see Rhodes et al., 2008) we considered that context pertained to variables such as the school performance, size, religious denomination, geographical location, and immediate environment in terms of an inner city, urban, sub-urban or rural location. In seeking contextual factors likely to be influential upon incumbent leadership actions and priorities, and hence potentially influential upon leadership talent needs and leadership development, the identification of school performance (improvement and effectiveness) and school size (complexity and opportunity) was used in guiding our selection of schools to be included in the sample. In addition to this we also sought a balance between primary and secondary schools in order to offer further enhancement of the range of possible responses offered by participants.

In qualitative research projects Thomas (2009) suggests that using the word 'sample', a word he associates with experimental research, does not always sit well with interpretive research, and that interpretative research has a credibility of its own without relying on samples which could be subject to such inferential statistical analysis as a more positivist approach may require. Denscombe (2003) also suggests that a small sample size is in keeping with the nature of qualitative research. Indeed, in practical terms, small numbers are more manageable because, for example, interviewing generally takes a great deal of researcher time in planning, travelling, executing and transcribing prior to analysis, when compared with the amount of time required to advance towards analysis upon receipt of the postal questionnaire returns. Devers and Frankel (2000) describe qualitative research design as a 'rough sketch' that must be filled in by the researcher. These authors also suggest that in developing the research design a researcher needs to understand and consider the unique characteristics of specific research respondents and the settings in which they are located. A sampling frame for the research sites and the research respondents is necessary here, and efforts to gain access will need to be made. They also say that in qualitative research purposive sampling is often at the heart of the sampling frame so that 'information rich' cases that provide the greatest insight into the research questions posed can be selected. In qualitative research, Lincoln and Guba (1985) remind us that samples may or may not be representative of any particular population engaged and may well focus on particular contexts and events which are not readily generalizable. Miles and Huberman (1994) suggest that 'cases' that are unusual or exceptional manifestations of the phenomenon of interest are potentially most revealing in purposive samples. However, it is incumbent upon researchers to be able to explain the basis for and use of purposive sampling and discuss any inherent implications for the research outcomes. Ball (1993) argues that people are the most complex aspect of such naturalistic sampling, given the complex social networks they belong to in organizations, thereby reminding us that identifying these often hidden connections so as to arrive at the key informants and gain their participation in the research demands skill on the part of the researcher. He also highlights the fact that participants may have their own concerns and cycles of behaviour depending on the activities they are engaged in, their own agendas, and their reasons for agreeing to be a participant. We must remember that sampling involves careful decision making about who the best informants are likely to be, and that our ideas may need to change once access has been granted and the research story unfolds.

Unit of analysis

Finally, in any sampling strategy as a researcher you will need to be aware of the sampling unit that is most appropriate to the intentions and purposes of your research. Knowing what the subject of interest is will help you determine whether an appropriate sampling unit is, for example, the entire organization, a group of organizations, a sub-section within an organization, similar teams in different organizations, or the members of a single team or some other unit. For example, if you were interested in the influence of life histories on the transition of individuals to headships, then your sampling unit would most likely be a group of headteachers and aspirant heads near transition who would meet your criteria stipulations. If however your interest was the power transactions within subject departments then your sampling unit would be those departments which met your criteria.

Gronn (2010) draws our attention to present thinking about the change taking place from individual 'heroic' leadership in educational settings, in which leadership is firmly located around a single person, to a more shared vision of leadership responsibilities. Although it is the case that senior leaders and those carrying the final responsibility and accountability for actions and outcomes still maintain a strong voice in contemporary educational settings, there is a strong recent trend towards distributing leadership, developing leadership teams, and encouraging talent pools for succession purposes. With this change in perspective comes new patterns of leadership practice, and so as a leadership researcher you will need to be clear about the which unit of analysis is appropriate to the nature and purposes of your research. For example, in studying leadership distribution is it the individual, a particular group, interacting individuals within groups, or the entire organization which should constitute an appropriate unit of analysis for your research?

Summary ☐

Researchers in educational leadership, as in other fields of research endeavour, will often have to rely upon samples to execute their projects and obtain data. In this chapter we have shown that it is important to define the population so a judgement of who belongs to it can be made, and hence also on what size and composition of sample might be appropriate. Careful planning of sampling at the design stage of a research project is vital. Access to research sites, securing the participation of individuals, ethical considerations and sampling strategy all need to be considered here. Whilst samples for qualitative studies are likely to be smaller than is the case for quantitative studies, care in securing enough of the right kind of respondents still pertains. The chapter offered some guidance and advice by presenting both theoretical and practical insights on how a sample may best be developed, and concluded with a reminder to researchers to consider the appropriate unit of analysis for the research intended.

Further reading

BERA (2011) *Ethical Guidelines for Educational Research*, British Educational Research Association. Available at www.bera.ac.uk

Cohen, L., Manion, L. and Morrison, K. (2011) *Research Methods in Education* (7th edition). London: Routledge.

Denscombe, M. (2010) *The Good Research Guide* (4th edition). Maidenhead: Open University Press.

Simons, H. (2009) *Case Study Research in Practice.* London: Sage.

Thomas, G. (2010) *How To Do Your Case-Study: A Guide for Students and Researchers.* London: Sage.

Questionnaire Research

Aims

This chapter aims to explore the strengths and weaknesses of using question-naires in leadership research. It begins by locating the use of questionnaires in relation to the your own philosophical stance towards knowledge and knowledge generation. By exploring the details of questionnaire planning and construction, the use of open and closed questioning and presentation, it aims to support you in creating questionnaires which have the potential to best fit your intended research project and secure appropriate data. Whilst questionnaires may be used in a survey as a single adopted method, they may also be used as part of a mixed-methods strategy. Whatever the strategy you deploy, the chapter aims to give you an opportunity to reflect upon the various procedures for administering questions and fostering a good response rate. In summary, we will try not only to assist you in deciding if your use of a questionnaire is appropriate but also in what type of questionnaire will be of use once its adoption is certain. (Details of the analysis of quantitative data such as that obtained by questionnaire use will be explored in Chapter 11.) By the end of this chapter you should be able to:

- plan and construct a questionnaire;
- understand the difference and relative merits of open and closed questions;
- see the advantages of mixed-methods research;
- perceive the advantages and disadvantages of mixed-methods research;
- understand the importance of good data collection processes and appropriate response rates.

Introduction

In pursuing a research project as a leadership researcher you may choose to focus on respondent stories (i.e. individual realities), with each of these set within their own unique context, and then seek to learn from these in all their detail and richness. This kind of phenomenological strategy is described by Denscombe (2003) and focuses much more on people's interpretations of events, hence giving rise to multiple realities that are shared by groups of people. In contrast, Trochim's post-positivist strategy (see Trochim and Donnelly, 2006), which by the way rejects the central tenets of positivism, argues that the purpose of social science research is to hold steadfastly to the goal of getting it right about reality, even though reaching that goal is impossible. In other words, this means arguing for a single but provisional shared reality that most people can subscribe to, although the perspectives and opinions of those who do not subscribe to such a shared reality must still be considered, and may also be significant.

Conversely, you may instead choose to adopt a more quantitative approach using questionnaires and thus utilize a more positivist strategy. Alternatively, a mixed-methods approach in which more than one method is used may be the best option if it serves your research objectives. Your underlying thinking in choosing a strategy that encompasses the methodology and methods adopted needs to be right. In short, a subjective or interpretivist stance is based upon a belief that reality and truth are a product of individual perception, and that knowledge is subjective and is based on experience and insight. A researcher adopting such a stance would normally opt for using qualitative methods, for example, interviews or focus groups. Conversely, an objective or positivist stance is based upon a belief that reality and truth are a 'given' and external to the individual, although there may be a shared reality that most people would subscribe to. In the positivist stance knowledge is thought to be hard and real, and capable of being transmitted in a tangible form. A researcher adopting such a stance would normally research using quantitative methods such as experiments, controlled trials and questionnaires. It is with the construction and use of questionnaires that this chapter addresses itself.

Once you develop an understanding of the research problem, the purpose of the research, the research design and the intended respondent population, it will then become necessary to consider which method(s) of data collection will best inform that research. Carefully choosing your method(s) for obtaining the best possible data fit for your intended research and its desired outcomes is essential. In considering your data collection, you are likely to consider your own philosophical stance as described above, the potential strengths of each method, which are most do-able, which constraints and opportunities present themselves, how the collected data may be analyzed, and whether you are able to perform such an analysis or are able to learn the techniques of analysis you seek to apply. Questionnaires, for example, are widely used for collecting survey data as they can offer a rapid, effective, efficient and confidential means of collecting a large number of responses, but you will need to be clear about exactly what it is you need to know because once your questionnaires are distributed there will be no going back. As an essential part of the planning and design of the intended research you must decide what type of questionnaire this will be.

Planning and constructing a questionnaire

A questionnaire survey can be used when the target population is generally large (see Chapter 5) and you are seeking quantitative data that will lend themselves to analysis using descriptive or inferential statistics (see Chapter 11). If the population is sufficiently large you will be able to analyze for responses from any sub-groups present within the sample. For example, responses could be compared between males and females or between senior leaders and classroom teachers. Although questionnaires may yield data which lack depth when compared to interview data, this does not preclude the use of some open-ended questions within a questionnaire to elicit more detailed textual responses. (This will be demonstrated later in the chapter.) As with other methods, questionnaires can contribute to cross-site and cross-level studies: for example, your research study could include staff in different local authorities, headteachers in a variety of schools located within the chosen authorities, and associated university-based education staff who work with those same headteachers in their schools. Munn and Drever (1996) describe a questionnaire as a written form of questioning, while Denscombe (2003) reminds us that authorisation to distribute questionnaires and conduct a survey will be needed from appropriate decision makers at the chosen research sites. Indeed some organizations, for example the health service, will have strict ethical codes about the questions or types of questions that may be asked.

Youngman (1994) argues that a successful questionnaire is one in which the types of data being gathered are related to a goal that is recognized well in advance. In addition, questionnaires need not to be particularly long, not too onerous, well-presented, and as interesting and accessible as possible to secure returns. Fowler (1998) points out that if a researcher is not present when questionnaires are completed, which may well be the case, this may lead to respondents not answering questions in a way that is useful to them. Again, careful questionnaire construction on the part of the researcher to ensure returns that will be of value is emphasized. For a postal questionnaire, provision of a covering letter or an introduction to explain the nature and purpose of the research, with clear contact and return details, reassurance concerning the ethical standards upheld, a pre-paid return envelope, and an acknowledgement with thanks for the time the respondent will take in completing and returning the questionnaire, could all help facilitate the provision of data. Note that you can help manage your questionnaire returns by attaching an appropriate identification number to each one. You can then use these identifiers for data entry onto a spread sheet prior to your analysis. Denscombe (2003) suggests offering respondents the most straightforward and least contentious questions at the start of the questionnaire and then increasing the complexity as the questions progress. Questionnaires often start with straightforward respondent details or demographic requests, such as invitations to state one's gender, sector of employment and the type of post held. Denscombe also advises avoiding words or phrases that may cause offence. Cohen et al. (2003) likewise suggest that the questions used in questionnaires should not be offensive or seek to mislead respondents, and caution that if the questions are potentially threatening or address an area of great sensitivity it may influence how those respondents answer. They remind us that a questionnaire is not just about promoting the researcher's agenda; rather it must also seek to capture the intended responses of participants. If a respondent is offered potentially threatening questions in an early part of the questionnaire, then they might be decide not to continue or make interpretations that will influence any later responses given. To minimize or avoid this unintended early influence, Cohen et al. suggest the following sequence:

1. Unthreatening factual questions.
2. Closed questions gaining responses on attitudes and opinions.
3. Open-ended questions seeking reasons for the responses given.

These authors also advocate that structured, semi-structured and unstructured questions may be used in questionnaire design. On this they offer the following advice:

> ... there is a simple rule of thumb: the larger the size of the sample, the more structured, closed and numerical the questionnaire may have to be, and the smaller the size of the sample, the less structured, more open and word-based the questionnaire may be. (2003: 247)

Advice concerning the construction of questionnaires appears frequently in the research literature. The final form will depend, of course, on the nature and purpose of your research and the sample of respondents who will receive the questionnaire. For example, the text you use will need to accommodate the experience and realistic levels of knowledge of the intended respondents, and any questions put to children for example will need to take this into account. Lambert (2008) examined the use of questionnaires in educational evaluation with very able pupils attending out-of-school classes. He suggested that materials need to be clear, concise and well-presented, and advises that researchers should always be open to questions from all those involved in the research whether this is pupils themselves or their parents. Appropriate behaviour and respect for the teacher's authority are also necessary when we are administering the questionnaires and interacting with pupils. Lambert added that questionnaires as a research instrument can appear invitingly deceptive, but cautioned on the potential complexity of the procedures involved from sending the materials to analysis of the data.

Piloting the questionnaire to try and increase the validity and trustworthiness of the research and its outcomes (see Chapter 3) will be valuable to you in all circumstances. It is usual to pilot a research instrument with a group of respondents drawn from the possible sample, but not to include the pilot group when completing the final version of the questionnaire. Piloting is useful in gaining assurance about the clarity and utility of the questions and the instructions given (note that your instructions will need to be exact on what to do: e.g. *put a tick* or *circle*), the appropriateness of their length, and that the completed pilots really do offer responses that are appropriate to the purposes of the research. You may need to make some revisions before you distribute your final version. The research literature frequently, and rightly, advises against using double questions, leading questions, presuming questions, hypothetical questions, over complex questions, double negative questions, and awkward questions. If you use multiple choice questions then your choices need to be discrete and must not overlap. If your questionnaires are not well constructed then a perfunctory response or even no response may be the result. A decision not to respond may be emphasized if the potential respondent frequently receives questionnaires from researchers (as is likely to be the case in many educational organizations). There may also be little or no opportunity for you to check on the accuracy or seriousness of the responses obtained (Robson, 1999) and there is no absolute certainty here that respondents will always respond truthfully (see Chapter 3). Thomas (2009: 174) comments on the possibility for 'prestige bias' to occur where, for example, in order to 'look good' or 'informed' or 'ethical', respondents may try and offer the 'right answer'. This author suggests that being aware that the potential for bias exists when constructing the questions, and emphasizing to the respondents that ethical standards including the right to anonymity will be upheld, may help diminish such prestige bias.

Open and closed questions

In seeking to obtain data using a questionnaire, your chosen questions may be 'closed' and will thus attract answers such as yes or no, or alternatively, your questions may be 'open-ended' and allow participants to respond in any way they wish. An advantage to using open-ended questions is that these allow the possibility for respondents to offer details that will be of value because they go beyond the potentially constraining list of options offered by the researcher. Conversely, an obvious disadvantage can be seen in the added complexity that comes in analyzing such responses, especially if the sample is large.

Using such scales can be helpful in establishing participants' attitudes or perceptions. Scales that are differentiated beyond seven possibilities of response may however require respondents to perceive differences which are unrealistic of the researcher to expect. Sometimes an odd number of choices

a. A Factual Two-Way or Dichotomous Response

Are you presently employed full time?   Yes

                                                                 No

b. Providing a list

List three benefits of collaboration:

c. Choosing an item from a list (where a single item can be chosen)

In working with a leadership coach, what do you value most?

    (i)   Achieving a trusting relationship
    (ii)   Receiving instructions
    (iii) Working with someone who has been in the job longer than you
    (iv) Receiving feedback

d. Multiple choice (where one or more choices can be asked of the respondent)

Which of the following topics could you teach at Master's level?

Human resource management
Strategic management
Research methods
Learning and learning contexts
Other   *please specify*_____

e. Category questions

How long have you been a college principal?

Less than 1 year
1–3 years
4–7 years
8+ years

f. Rank order questions from a list based upon a chosen criterion

Why did you choose this particular leadership course?

(Please place the list of points in rank order with the highest priority being 1.)

To help my employment potential
It is offered on an evening
Location
It was offered at a low cost

In rank ordering it assumes that respondents can differentiate their responses and make clear distinctions between offered statements.

g. Rating or Likert scales

Please tick one column to show your response.

Question	Strongly Agree	Agree	Undecided	Disagree	Strongly Disagree
Student voice should be used to inform leadership decision making					

More examples of question formats	No View	Respondents Indicating Importance or High Importance	Respondents Indicating Neutrality	Responding Indicating Low Importance or No Importance	P	Significance
Shows initiative	3	426	0	0	0.000	Significant
Has vision	1	425	3	0	0.000	Significant
Shows confidence	4	411	12	2	0.000	Significant
Has people skills	0	427	2	0	0.000	Significant
Is a competent teacher	9	344	59	17	0.000	Significant

(Characteristics of leadership talent modified from Rhodes et al., 2008)

h. Semantic Differential (often uses opposing adjectives and a seven-point scale)

Place a tick in the space below to show your view of school packed lunches

Nutritious	- - - - - - -	Unhealthy
Expensive	- - - - - - -	Inexpensive
Big	- - - - - - -	Small
Spicy	- - - - - - -	Bland
Exciting	- - - - - - -	Boring

i. Constant Sum or Points Distribution method

Please distribute 100 points between the choices shown below. Distribute these as you wish, but the final sum must add up to 100.

What for you are likely to be the key characteristics of leadership talent?

The possession of a whole school vision
The possession of good people skills
The respect of pupils
The ability to work to tight deadlines
To show consistency in decision making

j. Matrices or Grids with Questions having the Same Answer Scale

With regard to your own development, how important are each of the following criteria to you in experiencing a professional development activity?

To do this, please use the scale 1 to 5 (where 1 is the least important and 5 is the most important).

Good clear handouts are provided	1 2 3 4 5
There is opportunity for individual work	1 2 3 4 5
There is opportunity for group discussion	1 2 3 4 5
That the development is related to your own professional context	1 2 3 4 5
That you are shown how this learning may be implemented	1 2 3 4 5

Figure 6.1 Examples of formats of closed questions

will be used as in the five-point Likert scale as illustrated. This allows for the identification of a central point where respondents may have no strong feelings and they can then express their neutrality about a particular item put to them. This central point of neutrality is sometimes called the 'neutral null hypothesis' (see below). Some researchers will opt for using even numbers of choices, such as a six-point scale, believing that this is more likely to force the respondent to make a decision about a particular item rather than take the 'easy' option of indicating neutrality if they are uncertain about how to answer.

In some of our own work pertaining to leadership talent and leadership development (see Rhodes et al., 2008), we adopted a five-point Likert scale with a central neutral null hypothesis which had been important in the subsequent analysis undertaken (see also Chapter 11). In this research 20 characteristics indicative of leadership talent were identified, based upon the responses of headteachers, middle leaders and classroom teachers from a sample of schools in England. What follows is an extract from this work:

> A total of 429 questionnaires were secured from 70 heads, 191 middle leaders and 168 classroom teachers, providing a potentially diverse data sample. Taking the neutral null hypothesis as 3 of the 5 point Likert scale, a Wilcoxon Signed Rank Test was used to establish, for each characteristic, whether the number of respondents responding below, equal to or above the median was significant. The level of significance was set at $p \leq 0.005$. Head, middle leaders and classroom teacher respondents confirmed that they perceived all 20 characteristics to be significant in contributing to the identification of leadership talent. An illustrative and reduced table below shows responses to only 5 of the characteristics that may be indicative of leadership talent.

Open-ended questions can sometimes prove valuable in site-specific case studies, as they can probe the details of the particular area of interest within

a. Example of an Open Question

Which personal skills do you think are important to include in your leadership record of achievement? *Please write in ...*

b. Example of an Open Question

Having identified your level of satisfaction with the professional development provided *please explain why you came to this decision ...*

Figure 6.2 Examples of open-ended questions

its context and potentially offer richer data and insights into the complexity of the area that is of interest.

Mixed-methods research

In reviewing positivist and interpretivist stances in research, Johnson and Onwuegbuzie (2004) highlight the historical divergence between these two apparently dissonant 'qualitative' and 'quantitative' paradigms. Importantly, they present a third paradigm based upon the use of 'mixed-methods research'. In the article they formally define mixed-methods research as:

> the class of research where the researcher mixes or combines quantitative and qualitative research techniques, methods, approaches, concepts or language into a single study. (2004: 17)

They also advocate the possibility of either mixing qualitative and quantitative approaches within or across the stages of the research process, or the use of a qualitative phase and a quantitative phase in the overall research study. Simple examples of mixing methods would be to undertake a questionnaire survey to inform a subsequent interview phase of research, or alternatively, to use a questionnaire survey following an interview phase in order to corroborate findings, or otherwise, with a wider audience of respondents. It is important that as researchers in the field we adopt a strategy which will best help us achieve our research objectives.

In later work, Johnson, Onwuegbuzie and Turner (2007) offered no fewer than 19 definitions of mixed-methods research derived from leading researchers. They also offered a helpful continuum depicting degrees of mixing from pure qualitative to pure quantitative as follows:

- Pure qualitative (qualitative dominant).
- Qualitative mixed (qualitative dominant).
- Pure mixed (equal status).
- Quantitative mixed (quantitative dominant).
- Pure quantitative (quantitative dominant).

The establishment of this third 'mixed research' paradigm has been well made. However, Symonds and Gorard (2010: 133), whilst noting that mixed methods as a methodological discipline has grown in popularity, suggest that mixed-methods research as a third paradigm must not be allowed to reinforce the binary positioning of the qualitative and quantitative paradigms. Indeed, these authors call for more methodological independence so that mixed-methods research does not become a prescriptive force stifling creativity in thinking around the three alternatives of quantitative, qualitative and mixed methods.

The advantages and disadvantages of using questionnaires

Munn and Drever (1996: 2) offer a straightforward series of advantages to using a questionnaire. In summary, these may be stated as:

- an efficient use of available time;
- allowing for respondent anonymity;
- the possibility of receiving a high return rate;
- the possibility to standardize questions to facilitate analysis.

In contrast, Munn and Drever (ibid.: 5) also suggest a series of disadvantages. In summary, these may be may be stated as:

- the information received tends to offer description rather than any deep explanation;
- the information received can be superficial given the communication 'distance' between researcher and respondent;
- sufficient time must be spent in proper preparation and piloting or the questionnaire may have limited usefulness.

As previously stated, questionnaires can offer a rapid, effective, efficient and confidential means of collecting a large number of responses. The data collected can lend themselves to quantitative analysis using descriptive or inferential statistics (see Chapter 11), and open-ended textual sections can give respondents greater freedom of expression and be useful in capturing additional and valuable data outside the closed questions set by a researcher. Questionnaires can be used to good effect as part of a mixed-methods strategy in leadership research.

Questionnaire data collection and response rate

Postal questionnaires
Questionnaires sent through the post may be directed to each individual, or perhaps distributed by a key figure or permission giver associated with the research site chosen. Following completion they may be collected in person or returned in a provided and ideally pre-paid envelope. Note that the return rate is important in establishing trustworthiness and in undertaking analysis (see below).

Telephone questionnaires
Telephone questionnaires involve asking respondents simple questions over the telephone. There is perhaps greater possibility in this kind of administration to

assist respondents with completing the questionnaire, but also the possibility of introducing bias if they are led in any way or not clear about what is being asked. Telephone questionnaires can give rapid returns from respondents at distance at a reasonable cost. Some researchers, with good reason, would be cautious of mixing telephone and postal responses without establishing good justification, as the methods can introduce their own particular biases and in this sense they are distinct rather than necessarily complementary. As with postal questionnaires, full permission from research sites and respondents is appropriate. Note that pre-preparation will go a long way to ensuring a response, as unexpected 'cold-calling' is rarely appreciated and may in some types of research be viewed as unethical.

Online web questionnaires

Given that access to online resources is now commonplace in many parts of the world, the use of online or web questionnaires has burgeoned in recent years. For example, Survey Monkey at www.surveymonkey.com is well known and will allow researchers to create and distribute a good quality basic questionnaire in a professional format: it will easily allow a questionnaire to be sent to 100 potential respondents. More complex and larger questionnaire surveys are also possible using online services, and some will also help with analysis once the returns have been secured. Note however that these services are likely to entail financial costs. A search online will reveal the services that are available.

In a recent paper, Wilson and Dewaele (2010) offered some insights on data collection through the use of web questionnaires within the field of second language acquisition and bilingualism. They presented two case studies of research designs based on online questionnaires, and reflected upon the fact that the samples obtained were more or less self-selected and not representative of the general population (see Chapter 5). However, they also concluded that this does not automatically invalidate subsequent analyzes despite some shortages of certain types of participants. In these cases, they had enough of the shortage participants to check that this did not go against general trends. Overall, they held that the potential benefits of web-based questionnaires could outweigh their limitations.

Response rate

In postal questionnaires it is advisable to include a letter to explain the purpose of your research and to state the ethical stance you have adopted, including confidentiality and anonymity with respect to the individual(s) and the institution(s) concerned. Your name and contact details will also be important for the respondents. Depending on the population and the pre-preparation, as well as ethical procedures including the maintenance of anonymity, you may need to contact respondents or institutions again to increase your return rate.

The response rate is vital in terms of trustworthiness and subsequent analysis. Verma and Mallick (1999) stated that an initial response rate of less than 20% may not provide sufficiently detailed data, while Gillham (2000) argued that a return rate of less than 30% could lead to uncertainty concerning validity. Low response rates may result in bias given that an insufficiently broad selection of the sample perspectives may be obtained. Smith and Bost (2007) suggest that well-presented and accessible questionnaires for the intended audience could result in higher response rates. As mentioned above, the research literature frequently references covering letters, follow-ups and assurances concerning ethics as being potentially influential in increasing return rates. A return from at least 30 individuals is frequently mentioned in the research literature as a minimum should the researcher intend to apply inferential statistics in the analysis of the data obtained (see Chapter 11). Cohen et al. (2003) consider that a response rate of 75% could be achievable given that follow-up reminders are used. Some researchers also offer inducements such as prizes to encourage respondents to return their completed questionnaire. A former EdD (Doctor of Education) student in Leaders and Leadership in Education, Dr Alan Kirsz, adopted a questionnaire survey of adult volunteers in the Scout Organization as a means of assessing what they knew and understood about leadership. The following extract from his thesis (Kirsz, 2007:110) mentions the use of a 'prize draw':

> The letter and questionnaire also mentioned the provision of volunteer inclusion in a prize draw for a gift token as an 'appropriate type of incentive' (Cohen et al., 2000:) and by means of thanking respondents for their time and efforts.

Mitchell (1998) offered some thoughts on improving mail survey responses from UK academics. He concluded that one of the best aids to improvement was the inclusion of an explanatory covering letter with the questionnaire. The main negative item was the questionnaire being over four pages long. He found that survey response rates varied widely across academic departments, ranging from 30–63%. He advocated maximizing inducements and minimizing negatives which hindered responses, so that financial efficiency and research effectiveness could be enhanced.

Summary ☐

Choosing research methods that are best fitted to your intended research project and its desired outcomes is of crucial and clearly falls within your remit as a researcher. Whether adopted as a single data collection method or as part of a mixed-methods strategy, questionnaire use has both advantages and disadvantages. In this chapter you were guided towards making choices about the suitability of questionnaires, and if used, how they may be constructed and administered to foster successful data collection. Gaining a sufficient return that gives you the right kind of information to address your research issues is at the heart of this success. The chapter also introduced ideas pertaining to trustworthiness, piloting, ethics and analysis. Overall, questionnaires can offer a rapid, effective, efficient, and confidential means of collecting a large number of responses.

Further reading

Blaikie, N. (2003) *Analyzing Quantitative Data: From Description to Explanation.* London: Sage.

Cohen, L., Manion, L. and Morrison, K. (2011) *Research Methods in Education* (7th edition). London: Routledge.

Creswell, J.W. (2008) *Research Design: Qualitative, Quantitative and Mixed Methods* (3rd edition). London: Sage.

Denscombe, M. (2010) *The Good Research Guide* (4th edition). Maidenhead: Open University Press.

Gillham, B. (2008) *Developing a Questionnaire* (2nd edition). London: Continuum.

Munn, P. and Drever, E. (2004) *Using Questionnaires in Small-scale Research: A Beginner's Guide.* Edinburgh: The Scottish Council for Research in Education.

Useful websites

Survey Monkey at www.surveymonkey.com

7

Interviews and Focus Groups

Aims

Interviews are used by many leadership researchers either as their main research tool, as a way of gathering some initial data to understand the general issues, or as a final research-gathering technique to deepen understanding and confirm previous research. Utilizing such an approach has an appeal based on its apparent simplicity and intimacy but there are many skills associated with the appropriate and successful use of this approach. This chapter will discuss the use of interviews in researching educational leadership and attempt to outline some of the advantages and pitfalls of different kinds of interviews including focus groups. By the end of this chapter you should be able to:

- understand the reasons why interviews are considered central to research in educational leadership;
- be able to differentiate between different types of interview and know which type of interview is most suitable for which project;
- have a clear overview of the main theoretical concepts associated with interviews;
- understand how to construct an interview schedule;
- know how to conduct an interview, and how to record what you hear;
- analyze the data gained from interviews;
- have a clear understanding of the merits and challenges of using focus groups.

Why interviews?

Interviews are undoubtedly one of the most popular research tools for those engaged in research in education generally, and educational leadership specifically. The reasons for this are complex, being partly pragmatic and relating to the skill sets possessed by many researchers, and partly theoretical and relating to the requirement to gain a depth of understanding of the topic under scrutiny in the complex work of educational institutions. It is sadly the case that comparatively few educational professionals will gain a strong grasp of the use of statistical techniques, and so utilizing quantitative methods is challenging if not impossible for many as a way of investigating educational leadership issues. By contrast, all teachers and lecturers are, by virtue of their nature and training, articulate and skilled at interaction with others since the very act of teaching requires high levels of expertise in human communication.

For these reasons, interviews are a natural method (probably *the* natural method) of undertaking research for most aspiring or expert researchers in the social sciences. However, the reason for using such an approach is not merely a lack of ability in other methods since interviews have a lot to commend them for use in many types of research project. As Kvale (2007) has noted, interviews are helpful since knowledge is often generated between humans through conversations. This is especially relevant to schools, colleges and universities since such institutions are fundamentally social in nature, and their activities relate to personal relationships that are built up in classrooms, staffrooms, meetings, offices and so on. If we are to understand the dynamics of these situations then one of the best ways of doing so is often to gather data by, to put it at its simplest, talking to the people involved to ask them about the topic under investigation. In this way we can swiftly gain large amounts of interesting and relevant material that will be highly germane to our area of interest, and may well offer the possibility of key insights that would not be possible to establish through the use of other techniques such as questionnaires or observation alone.

Do remember however that as a researcher you will need to accept that interviews pose challenges, in that they require high levels of skill if they are to be managed effectively and preparation is needed beforehand if they are to be successful in gaining the maximum amount of useful data. It is also important to remember that interviews are neither exclusively subjective nor objective but intersubjective, since both the interviewer and the interviewee will bring their perspectives to bear on the topic under discussion. In this sense interviews allow all participants to discuss their own interpretations of the world and talk about situations using their own point of view (Cohen et al., 2007: 349). This means that it is inevitable that both the conduct of the interview and the process of analysis may be influenced or biased by the interviewer's own views. For this reason, it is always difficult as a researcher to argue for the generalizability and universality of research findings that are based solely on interviews. It is for this reason that Robson argues that the interview is really an effective substitute for ethnographic research, since the linguistic interchange embodied in the interview approach can open a virtually unique window on what lies behind our actions (Robson, 2006: 272). Note that there are many books that focus solely on how to prepare for and how to conduct interviews, one of the most useful of which remains that by Drever (1995) which explains concisely how to construct and carry out an interview.

The delivery format

A variety of formats are available for interviewing, including face-to-face, telephone, video conferencing and online interviews. In general, face-to-face interviews are considered the best approach wherever possible because the interviewer can interact with the interviewee and note their full response, including their tone of voice, manner, body language, and so forth. However, there will be certain circumstances where constraints of time, finance or whatever will make it difficult or impossible for you to meet with some or all of your respondents in person, and in such circumstances the only approach open to you may be to use some form of electronic communication. Despite the constraints that this approach may place on the process such interviews can still be a very valuable form of data gathering, and this kind of interview can be especially useful when you need to undertake a large number of brief interviews comparatively swiftly. Tables 7.1 and 7.2 show some of the types and formats of interviews that can be used.

You will find that each approach offers certain advantages but also poses challenges. Electronic forms of interview mean that a wide range of people can be interviewed swiftly and with comparative ease at a low cost. Indeed, there

Table 7.1 Interview formats (based on Burton et al., 2008: 83–86)

Type of interview	Methods	Advantages and disadvantages
F2F (face-to-face)	The 'traditional' format for interviews where the interviewer and interviewee pre-arrange a date, time, place and focus for the interview.	Generally most effective when the interviewer goes to the interviewee, particularly if it is 'neutral ground'. Convenient for the interviewee and avoids distractions.
Video conferencing	The interview takes place using a video link that is secure and so ensures confidentiality.	Means that more geographically distant potential respondents can be approached, may save on travel time and costs, can be an expensive option and does require that both 'ends' of the interview have the necessary technology and skills available to them.
Telephone interview	The interview takes place using a normal telephone line at a time agreed between the interviewer and interviewee.	Generally easy to arrange and very convenient, but does not allow for the observation of physical cues and mannerisms.
Online	Use of a web-based 'chat room' as the interview location.	Increasingly popular as researchers and respondents become more familiar with and reliant on digital technology and ICT. Confidentiality and safety need to be ensured.

are many circumstances where problems of time and finance mean that the only viable option is to use telephone, video or internet approaches. However, all of these means lack the level of personal contact which can be essential for a really successful interview, where an understanding of non-verbal cues and a calm and friendly atmosphere can help to ensure that the best data are gained. For this reason, the immediacy and intimacy of a face-to-face interview remains the best way to undertake interviews where it is possible to do so. Nonetheless, many projects would not be viable and much valuable data would remain uncollected if electronic means were not used. Note that there is also something of a generational issue here as well, since many people are now so used to communicating online that this has become a 'natural environment' in its own right, and there may now be a great many respondents who would be at least as open online as in face-to-face situations. The most important thing is that both the interviewer and the interviewee will need to be confident and comfortable with the format and with all the surrounding circumstances of the interview, including where it takes place (even if virtually), that confidentiality is ensured, and that it is made clear that openness and honesty are required.

Types of interview

Interviews are really only appropriate for small samples, since their conduct is time consuming and can be costly in terms of travelling to and from interview sites, but do remember that their greatest strength lies in the fact that very large amounts of data can be gathered during each interview and the level of detail and quality of that material can be considerable. In this sense, interviews are almost unique in the richness of data that can be gathered.

The three main types of interview

- *Unstructured interviews* – where the interviewer simply engages with the respondent on the topic he or she is interested in, with no predefined agenda, and allows the interview to take whatever course it may.
- *Semi-structured interviews* – where the interviewer has a series of predefined questions under main headings, but allows some degree of latitude in what is discussed.
- *Structured interviews* – where the interviewer asks only a series of predefined and detailed questions, and allows little or no latitude in exploring the wider issues.

As shown in Table 7.2, each of these approaches has its merits and demerits and each one is more or less suitable for different purposes.

Whichever approach you choose, considerable preparation is not only recommended but also essential if the interview is to be successful in developing the right kind of relationship between you and the interviewee, one that will ensure you gather as much relevant data as possible.

Table 7.2 Types of interview

Unstructured	Allows the respondent to discuss a wide range of issues more or less under their own control with only light guidance from the interviewer. Can produce very rich and detailed data and allow issues to emerge as the conversation develops.	Can have a tendency to meander and lead to convoluted discussions that are not necessarily on topic. Can be difficult to manage and may lead to gathering a great deal of irrelevant data.	Useful in certain types of research such as grounded theory or ethnographic approaches where the researcher does not have any clear preconceived ideas about what they expect to find.
Semi-structured	Enables the researcher to guide the interview and ensure that the respondent addresses the key issues that have been defined in the interview schedule. Produces rich data on the topic under scrutiny.	Can lack spontaneity and may cause problems for the researcher in trying to keep the respondent on topic. Issues that may be relevant but were not included in the interview schedule may also be missed.	Useful in most situations where there is plenty of time to plan the interview and where the discussion can take place in a relaxed and private atmosphere.
Structured	Allows the researcher to gather a wide range of key data very swiftly according to preconceived questions.	Only allows for short questions and answers on questions identified before the interview. Comparatively little rich data are likely to be elicited, and both the interviewer and respondent may feel that much has been left unexplored.	Can be very helpful when trying to gather data on very specific questions that require brief answers, such as ages, preferences, roles, etc. Has the advantage of speed and clarity of purpose, and can often be undertaken very quickly in ad hoc situations such as corridors, classrooms, and rest areas. Some of the resulting data may be suitable for basic statistical analysis.

Constructing the interview schedule

As we said previously the one major advantage of interviews is their adaptability (Bell, 2005:157), by which we mean that they can be used to explore a very wide range of issues and gain a great a deal of data very swiftly. However, 'a great deal' will depend on your ability as the interviewer to pose appropriate questions and respond to the answers an interviewee gives, and then to take the interview forward as a result of their responses. To do this successfully you will need to:

- possess, and possibly demonstrate, considerable background knowledge;
- use informed questioning (based on the ideas and research findings from previous reading);
- react with sensitivity to new leads (adapted from Burton et al, 2008: 87).

An *interview schedule* is a document prepared by the interviewer prior to the interview which outlines the questions that will be asked in the interview itself. It is generally considered good practice to provide the interviewee with the interview schedule prior to the event, so that they are aware of the questions that will be asked and can give some thought to their responses. There is an art to preparing a good interview schedule, and how you formulate this document can predetermine the likelihood of a successful outcome. Note that it will often prove helpful if the first section of the document outlines the key issues that will need to be dealt with prior to asking the actual questions, such as:

- the title of the research;
- the time and place of the interview;
- the name of the respondent (or number if this is preferred).

It is also good practice to have a standard preamble which you will read to the interviewee explaining the nature of the interview and the reasons why it is taking place. This will also offer guarantees about anonymity (where agreed) and the security of the data.

The way that the subsequent questions which make up the main body of the document are posed can predetermine the kind of response you receive. Up to seven different kinds of question and response have been identified (Tuckman, 1972) but the main and crucial differentiation that is usually made is between *closed* and *open* questions. 'Closed' questions tend to limit the possible responses of the interviewee and are most appropriate when trying to find out simple, factual information, such as asking how long a respondent has been in post, the number of students on roll, how many colleagues are in a certain department, and so on. By contrast 'open' questions will encourage a respondent to be expansive in their responses, and are likely to involve invocations such as 'Tell me about ...' or 'What is your view ...?', etc. Closed questions are likely to prove most relevant in short, structured interviews, while open questions are likely to form the majority of the interaction in a semi-structured or unstructured interview. However, the range of types of question involved in an interview can be very subtle and different types of questions can be identified that will:

- introduce the theme of the study to the interviewee;
- ask for information;
- ask for an example;
- probe and follow up a response;
- interpret and reformulate a response (clarify and check understanding) (Kvale 1996: 133–135).

All of these kinds of question can be integrated into a successful interview and, as the list above suggests, the order in which they are asked can be very important.

The way you phrase questions will thus be crucial to the outcome of the meeting, but the number and ordering of questions is also vital. In a semi-structured interview lasting an hour it is unlikely that you will explore any more than about five or six themes in any detail, and so your schedule should naturally fall into five or six sections. The order of these sections can be very important and so you should give considerable thought to which approach you should adopt. The first section of the interview should be used to gain any simple, relevant material that may only require brief, precise answers, such as length of time in post, main role of the respondent, previous roles etc. Such material can be dealt with swiftly and will allow your respondents to become engaged in the interview prior to any more detailed or reflective questions. The subsequent sections of the interview should be based on the major issues that are to be explored in some detail. Denscombe (2003:179) suggests a process of questioning that links prompts, probes and checks to interviewer behaviours, since the interviewer can encourage the interviewee to respond by remaining silent, repeating the question or the last few words of the response, or asking for examples.

Typically, each section may contain only one or two main questions with possible follow-up questions. Such questions must fit into three categories:

- *Main questions* – which address the major issue under scrutiny and allow the respondent the broadest latitude for response. Such questions are intended to be open-ended and to invite the respondent to reflect and respond at length.
- *Probes* – which are follow-up questions designed to explore issues in more detail.
- *Prompts* – which are simple and often quite direct questions whose aim is to gain some data on key issues where the respondent has not addressed these matters in their response to the main question or the probe question. Such questions are far less open and will literally 'prompt' the interviewee for a response.

Some interviewers prefer not to use prompts at all since they may skew respondents' responses towards the 'message' stated in the question itself. Indeed it is generally good practice to only use probes and prompts where the interviewee feels that insufficient data has been gathered by the use of the main question. A number of factors will affect the quality of the response to the questions, including:

- the skill with which the main question is constructed;
- the manner in which the interview is conducted;
- the background and personal characteristics of the respondent, some of whom will naturally be more inclined towards an open and frank discussion than others.

It is generally held that educated and articulate respondents are more likely to converse openly and in detail. For this reason you may well find that interviews with professional colleagues are often the most productive, and the key skill can lie in moving on from one theme to another rather than in eliciting an initial response.

The themes that underpin the questions in the sections of the schedule can be derived from a number of sources, including:

- your initial reading of previous research and ideas on the topic (the initial literature review);
- other sources of data gathering, such as your initial questionnaire, observations, field notes etc.;
- your previous professional experience as an interviewer;
- the content of relevant publications and documents, such as national, regional or local policy documents, laws etc. This can be especially important when the purpose of the interview is to test out some current or proposed policy.

Crucially, the questions that you ask should relate closely to the main aims of the study. The reasons for this are self-evident since gathering data on issues that are not directly related to what you are trying to test out or discover will be of little use. However, structuring your questions very closely in relation to your aims can have many other benefits, because this approach can make your subsequent data presentation and analysis simpler and help give structural integrity to your final report. This is because such an approach can allow you to compose the content of your main aims, and then structure the literature review around the key themes derived from these aims, employ the same themes in constructing the interview schedule, and finally analyze and present your findings according to the same issues. This can also make your analysis much simpler since you can readily reflect back on your aims and the literature that you accessed previously when analyzing the data from the interviews. You can then use this same approach when writing up your research report, dissertation or thesis, thus adding a level of readability and accessibility that would otherwise not have been the case. Note however that such an approach is not always possible, either because your questions cannot be derived directly and simply from your aims or because your research approach is one where the aims are general since you want themes to emerge from the data. This 'system' is certainly the simplest though, and is one that often underpins many professional research projects. Figure 7.1 shows an example of a semi-structured interview schedule used with headteachers to explore the topic of curriculum innovation. Note the overall structure of the document and the use of probes and prompts as well as main questions.

Research Project: Leading Curriculum Innovation in Schools
Headteacher Interviews

Respondent:
Date: **Time:**
Interview location:

Introduction
Thanks you again for letting me interview you. As you know, the project focuses on leading curriculum innovation. There are three key areas of research investigation, including the kinds of successful curriculum innovation that is taking place in schools, how such change is managed, and the impact such change can have on outcomes. The interview will focus on these main issues. As you are aware I would like to record the interview, but of course you have the right not to agree this request and you can stop me at any time if you wish to suspend or end the interview.

Section 1: Context
Main question 1.1: Please tell me a little about yourself. For instance, when did you become a headteacher and how long have you been in your present post?
Main question 1.2: What is the current context of the school? For instance, how many pupils are on the roll, how many staff do you have, and what is the social context of the children who attend?
Main question 1.3: What do you see as the key challenges for the school currently and in the future?

Section 2: Changes to the curriculum already implemented
Main question 2.1: You have already made changes to the curriculum in your school. Can you describe the circumstances/catalyst which triggered the decision to make changes to your school's curriculum and roughly when you began the process of change?
Probe: What were the problems along the way? What worked best and had the greatest impact on the school and on outcomes?
Prompts: Were there problems with staff who did not want to make changes to the curriculum? Were you constrained by resource implications? Were parents and governors supportive?

Main question 2.2: Could you outline the key changes which have taken place in relation to three areas: the way in which the curriculum is organized; the changes to the way staff are used to deliver the curriculum; and any changes in management structure to help in curriculum delivery and innovation?
Probe: Have you had to reorganize the curriculum and staffing or employ new staff to make the innovations you wanted?
Prompts: Did you need to employ new staff or retrain current staff? Were your deputies and heads of department supportive?

Section 3: Managing curriculum change
Main question 3.1: Some schools find curriculum innovations very difficult to manage in a way which ensures success. You have led successful curriculum innovation in your school. Could you identify some of the strategies and skills you have used to bring this about?
Probe: What was the hardest thing to manage in the process? Do you think that the changes can be sustained? What was the greatest help in the process? Did you need external support?
Prompts: Did you rely on certain key staff such as the senior management team or heads of year, etc.? Were external consultants or advisers a help? To what extent did you have to lead change yourself and how did you do so?

Main question 3.2: How do you think curriculum innovation can be encouraged and developed in challenging circumstances in your school as well as in other circumstances?
Probe: To what extent do you think the context and background of students is important? What role does staff training and development play in the process?

(Continued)

Figure 7.1 (Continued)

Prompt: Can innovation be carried out without better training? How important is it that staff work together as a team? How far do you have to mentor staff to make change possible?

Section 4: Evidence of impact
Main question 4.1: The research project is concerned to identify some best practice in CI. What would you say most clearly identifies best practice in your school?
Probe: Does learning and teaching seem to have improved? Are relationships between staff and pupils better?
Prompts: Are key areas of learning such as literacy and numeracy improving? Do staff comment positively on student's attitudes and achievements? Is pupil voice listened to more attentively and are students more involved in the life of the school?

Main question 4.2: What evidence do you have that innovation has led to enhanced outcomes?
Probe: Have the results of internal and external assessment improved? If so, to what extent and which areas have improved the most?
Prompt: Can you give me specific examples of raising levels of attainment in terms of examination and assessment results?

Closing statement: Those are all of the questions that I have for you and we have reached the end of the session. Thank you for agreeing to be interviewed. I would emphasize once again that everything you have said will be kept in the strictest confidence. I will be in touch with you again in the near future with a transcript of our meeting, and I would be grateful if you would read through the document and make any amendments to it that you feel appropriate, where you feel that you misstated issues, or where the transcript is not clear about what was said. Do you have any final questions or issues that you would like to raise about the interview?

Figure 7.1 Interview schedule for interviews with headteachers during curriculum innovation project

Recording the interview

Care must be taken in your choice of recording techniques, and you should always agree this in advance with individual interviewees since some will be happy with certain types of approaches and not others. Note that while most will agree to have some form of electronic recording of their interview, some will only allow the use of note-taking. Clearly, the format for the interview may determine the best approach to recording, since video-conferencing and internet communication can be video or audio recorded whereas telephone conversations are only suitable for an audio format. Face-to-face meetings can be suitable for videoing but such an approach is cumbersome in terms of setting up equipment, and this kind of interview can be very intimidating, leading to a loss of spontaneity and detail. However, there will be some circumstances where you will deem video-recording essential because of the nature of your research.

Overall, audio recording remains the most common approach since it is simple to operate and unobtrusive, but allows for the collection of a large volume of material speedily, and in such a way that it can be played back and transcribed with comparative ease provided the sound quality is good. Tape recording still remains popular with some researchers but digital audio recording is becoming increasingly ubiquitous, since digital recorders are comparatively inexpensive and offer excellent sound quality. The consequent audio files can be played back on the recording device itself or imported into personal computers and subsequently shared with other researchers in the research team: these can then be stored simply and safely, taking up no physical space whatever.

Contemporaneous note-taking will inevitably split your concentration as interviewer between the actual process of writing down what has been said and the conduct of the interview, and will only produce a partial record unless you are a very skilled note-taker or adept at shorthand. Such notes will be based upon what appears to be important to you at the time and may not record all of the very important issues, thus biasing the subsequent data and final report towards your personal predilections and beliefs rather than being based on the actual material the interviewee was trying to communicate. Despite such drawbacks this approach should not be dismissed since, as stated earlier, some interviewees will only agree to note-taking and so this may be the only way to gather any data at all. Even if video or audio recording is taking place most of us will still like to take some notes, since as researchers we can never be certain about the quality of the sound recording until after the meeting and playback has taken place. In addition, contemporaneous notes can help us to record the key issues that appear to be emerging and note new themes that might be explored later in the interview or in subsequent interviews. Such notes can also assist in subsequent analysis since they can indicate points in the interview that appear to be central to the issues under scrutiny, and which we might then identify in the audio recording as requiring special attention. For most interviewers the development of a good note-taking technique that does not distract too much from the conduct of the interview, but allows for the recording of salient points, is a skill which will develop over time and during a number of interviews. This is one of the many reasons why a new or early career researcher would be wise to conduct a trial or pilot study prior to the main data-gathering.

Good note-taking can be aided by the way in which the interview schedule itself is constructed. Figure 7.2 illustrates one approach to the development of an interview schedule where only the main questions are shown. Alternatively, the questions can be placed in a column which takes up only half of the schedule – the concept here is that notes can be made either beside or below the questions themselves, on the actual schedule. This has the advantage of ensuring that only key points are recorded, and that these are noted against the questions themselves as they are asked. Some researchers find this very helpful in developing their skills in identifying key points, but others will experience a certain amount of frustration in the lack of space and will either use only blank paper or have additional sheets of paper available. Note however that care needs to be taken not to make the process more, rather than less, cumbersome.

The timing and manner of the interview

Your 'manner' as an interviewer is important in all forms of interview, in terms of putting interviewees at ease and encouraging them to discuss the issue in question with openness and confidence. It is vital that interviewees are calm throughout the meeting and encouraged to speak about the issue at hand, but not 'over-encouraged' to such an extent that they may magnify this or seek to place an emphasis on certain topics because they feel these are of special interest to you as interviewer. On occasions interviewees may betray confidences or touch on topics that are distressing or problematic in a variety of ways. You will then have to judge when to challenge an interviewee but, crucially, you will also have to

Research Project: Leading Curriculum Innovation in Schools.
Teacher Interviews
Respondent:
Date: **Time:**
Interview location:

Introduction
Thanks you again for letting me interview you. As you know, the project focuses on leading curriculum innovation. There are three key areas of research investigation including the kinds of successful curriculum innovation that is taking place in schools, how such change is managed, and the impact such change can have on outcomes. The interview will focus on these main issues. As you are aware, I would like to record the interview but of course you have the right not to agree this request and you can stop me at any time if you wish to suspend or end the interview.

Section 1: Context
Main question 1.1: Please tell me a little about yourself. For instance when did you take up your current role and how long have you been in your present post?

Main question 1.2: What is your current role? How subjects do you teach, which students do you work with and what sort of backgrounds do they come from, and what is the current level of attainment?

Main question 1.3: What do you see as the key challenges for the school and for you as a teacher currently and in the future?

Section 2: Changes to the curriculum already implemented
2.1 Main questions: Can you tell me a little about the curriculum changes which have taken place recently at the school and how they have impacted on you as a class teacher?

2.2 Main questions: What areas of curriculum innovation and change have you been involved in personally or as part of a team with others? What role have you taken in the implementation of change and how has this impacted on your work?

Section 3: Managing curriculum change
3.1 Main questions: How have you been involved in the school's changes to the curriculum – because we are interested in the process of change and how this is experienced by teachers? (Eg. Training days, staff meetings, intranet communications, attendance at key decision making meetings/sharing of classroom practice across the school).

3.2 Main questions: Do you feel ready to begin implementing the recommendations for change embodied in recent government initiatives? Could you identify any skills development which you and other colleagues require in order to implement a revised curriculum?

Section 4: Evidence of impact
4.1 Main questions: What evidence do you have of curriculum change leading to better outcomes for students? How far can this be evidences by improvements in external assessment? Can you give specific examples drawn from school data? Are there examples of certain types of student who have benefited most from curriculum innovation?

4.2 Main questions: To what extent has the curriculum change assisted you in your teaching? How have relationships with students developed or changed? What do you feel are the main advantages and disadvantages of the changes that have taken place?

Closing statement: Those are all of the questions that I have for you and we have reached the end of the session. Thank you for agreeing to be interviewed. I emphasise once again that everything that you have said will be kept in the strictest confidence. I will be in touch with you again in the near future with a transcript of our meeting and I would be grateful if you would read through the document and make any amendments to it you feel appropriate where you feel that you misstated issues or where the transcript is not clear about what was said. Do you have any final questions or issues that you would like to raise about the interview?

Figure 7.2   Alternative interview schedule for interviews with headteachers during curriculum innovation project

remain calm and seek not to betray any sense of 'judgement' on what is being confided. If the interview becomes distressing for any of those involved all parties must retain the right to suspend or curtail the meeting. Effective interviewing is a skill that must be developed over time, and it is often only after a number of interviews on any given topic or project, when you have become really familiar both with the issues and the schedule, that the process becomes efficient.

In-depth interviews will usually take around an hour to conduct, but you may need additional time to set up recording devices and prepare for subsequent interviews. However, if you are conducting a large number of interviews where comparatively small amounts of data will be required from each respondent (often structured interviews), then much shorter interactions may be appropriate that could last a few minutes each.

Focus groups

Focus groups have become an increasingly popular way of gathering data and they are included here since they are, in essence but not solely, a form of interview carried out with multiple respondents. The distinctive characteristics of this approach are:

- focus groups involve homogeneous people in social interactions;
- the purpose of the focus group is to collect qualitative data from focused discussion;
- focus group interviewing is a qualitative approach to gaining information that is both inductive and naturalistic (adapted from Krueger and Casey, 2000: 18).

This technique will allow you to develop an understanding of why people feel a certain way, and participants can bring up issues which they feel are important rather than just responding to your questions. The technique also allows individuals to respond to each other to build on or contradict previous replies, so strong interactions can take place which may provide you with especially interesting data. Perhaps most significantly, the focus group approach will allow you to gather a very large amount of data with a considerable number of participants very swiftly (Bryman, 2004: 348). However, the elements that give strength to the focus group approach can also give rise to some serious problems. For instance, focus groups can be notoriously hard to manage:

- There is a danger that the group will be unresponsive and the researcher may be faced with a lengthy period of little or no interaction.
- In the obverse, robust interactions may get out of hand and the researcher may find it difficult to manage a group of people, or individuals within that group, who are combative or intolerant of other people's perspectives.
- Planning the questioning can be challenging since the researcher needs to encourage the group to focus on the topic, discuss the issue openly and calmly, and interact appropriately.

For all of these reasons you may wish to follow some basic advice:

- Select your participants carefully and try to make sure that there is an appropriate mix of people representing various relevant groups, taking account of the balance of gender, ethnic background, age groups etc.
- Be careful to keep the size of the group manageable (a minimum of four people and a maximum of twelve is often best).
- Work out your questions very carefully in advance and try to make these develop one to the other so that the topic can be moved forward.
- Make the ground rules for the session very clear prior to the commencement of the actual discussion.
- Intervene swiftly if the interaction is becoming heated and try to keep the group 'on track'.
- Always record the session using a digital or tape recorder, since making notes is inadvisable if not impossible unless more than one researcher is involved.

If these basic ground rules are adhered to this can be a very useful addition to your armoury as a qualitative researcher, but the focus group approach should not be adopted without a careful consideration of its merits and challenges.

Summary ☐

Interviewing remains one of the most common approaches to research on educational leadership. This is partly because most researchers are themselves from a background in education and have a natural tendency to be skilled at verbal interaction with colleagues. It is also because the interview, of whatever type, offers the opportunity to explore a topic in depth and in confidence, and to range across a variety of issues in such way as to produce a large volume of relevant data. It is critical that you choose the format of the interview carefully and develop an interview schedule that will allow the key themes to be explored as fully as possible in the time available.

The skills required for conducting interviews are complex and multifaceted and it is only with experience and confidence that you will be able to carry out really good interviews. Good preparation, allied to the development of positive relationships with interviewees, will be the key to having successful outcomes.

Further reading

Gilbert, N. (2003) *Researching Social Life.* London: Sage.

Kamberelis, G. and Dimitriadis, G. (2013) *Focus Groups: From Structured Interviews to Collective Conversations.* London: Sage.

Roulston, K.J. (2010) *Reflective Interviewing: A Guide to Theory and Practice.* London: Sage.

Seidman, I. (2006) *Interviewing as Qualitative Research: A Guide for Researchers in Education and the Social Sciences.* New York: Teachers College Press.

Silverman, D. (2004) *Qualitative Research: Theory, Method and Practice.* London: Sage.

Silverman, D. (2005) *Doing Qualitative Research.* London: Sage.

8

Using Observation

Aims

Observation can be one of the most powerful tools available for research in educational leadership, and the training and experience of those engaged in educational management make this approach especially relevant since such roles require close attention to the details of professional context in order to monitor institutional effectiveness. For instance, educational leaders and managers at all levels must constantly monitor student progress in relation not only to their academic development but also to the progress of their wider skills and behaviours, such as the development of socialization in schools or readiness for work and the professions in colleges and universities. Professional educators will quite naturally observe and monitor students on a regular basis in order to make sure that their methods of teaching are effective and that students are engaged with the materials presented to them. The rise of national regimes of accountability, such as the inspection systems for schools, colleges and universities that are operant in many countries, is based on a methodology that has at its heart a process of systematic observation to judge the quality of individual teachers and lecturers and educational institutions as a whole. Increasingly, institutions and their leaders are also employing observation as part of mentoring and coaching activities or for performance reviews. It therefore follows that educational professionals should have the prerequisite skills to ensure that observation is employed to good effect, and many research projects in education can integrate observation as one of the research tools that will form an overall methodology.

By the end of this chapter you should be able to:

- understand the power of observation as a research approach;
- recognize the strengths and weaknesses of observation and the recording of observations to determine the appropriateness of the approach;
- construct observation schedules suitable to the context and the conceptual focus of the research.

The power of observation as a research tool

In much the same way as we have argued that interviews are often a 'natural' research tool for those engaged in educational research, the use of observation comes comparatively easily to many, if not all, of those undertaking research in educational settings. Yet we have also argued elsewhere that it remains surprising how infrequently observation forms part of the research methodology. There are three main reasons for this:

1. The reluctance to integrate observation into a research project is a hang-over from notions that research should be 'scientific' in character, and many researchers seem to feel that simply looking at what is going on around them will not be viewed as 'good research'. This is, of course, somewhat ironic, since observation has been central to the scientific method, especially in the biological sciences, for hundreds of years.
2. 'Familiarity breeds contempt', and many aspirant researchers will be reluctant to use a research tool which they employ every day in their professional lives, sometimes quite understandably, because they wish to try out other less familiar and more esoteric research techniques.
3. There is often a concern that observational approaches will be time-consuming and that research tools will be complex and difficult to develop. Again, this last point is quite understandable since the kind of unstructured everyday observation that practitioners undertake as part of their work may not seem appropriate for a formal research project which may have both money and personal prestige invested in it.

Although all of these concerns are valid the lack of attention paid to the use of observation as a research technique is a great shame since observation can, as we have already noted, be used as part of any number of research approaches, and is also one of the most flexible ways to conduct research. For instance, comparatively unstructured observation can be employed as part of a highly qualitative methodology and is one of the bases of ethnography, and it can also be employed as part of many of the other more interpretive approaches such as grounded theory or phenomenology. However, the use of observation need not be confined to qualitative research since systematic observation can elicit data that are susceptible to the use of statistical analysis as a means of calculating frequencies. Such an approach may be very appropriate for educational leaders since it can generate generalizable conclusions about events that may assist in the analysis of learning success or failure, behaviour modification, or socialization, adaptation and change management. Observation can also be employed as one element of a mixed-methods approach and may, for instance, be used as a first research tool that will provide the basis for subsequent positivist research tools, or as a second or third research tool that will add richness to the data-gathering process. For this reason many researchers will carry out observations at the start of the data-gathering in order to gain initial insights into the research topic, and will then use the themes or issues they unearth as a basis for developing subsequent questionnaires. In the obverse a questionnaire approach might be used initially to gather a broad conception of the issues from a large sample, and then observation may be employed to gain deep, rich data that explore the issues in more detail. Finally, observation can be operated simultaneously with other research approaches and thus allowed to both inform and be informed by other data-gathering techniques. The next section will explore these issues in more depth.

The uses of observation

If we examine some of the advantages and disadvantages of this approach we may note that observation can reveal rich data on behaviours, characteristics and group interactions that the researcher and subjects may not themselves be aware of, but it can be time-consuming and lengthy, and subjective in interpretation. It is especially appropriate for examining teacher-student or student-to-student interactions in classroom, lecture or social situations, but it can also be used to examine colleague-to-colleague interactions or relationships between colleagues and clients, parents etc. As an approach it is most commonly employed within a qualitative methodology but, as noted above, observation schedules can include carefully thought-out mapping techniques that are susceptible to quantitative analysis (Burton and Brundrett, 2005; Burton et al., 2008).

Observation is especially helpful in providing deep, rich data that give verisimilitude to the research process since 'it provides a degree of life experience that is lacking in most academic environments' (Hammersley, 1993a: 197). Thody (2006: 133) suggests that observation is especially useful in the 'openings' to research reports since it is unrivalled in attracting reader attention and in establishing the atmosphere of the context within which the research took place. Whether used as an opening that leads on to other types of data collection and analysis or as the totality of the method employed, it is undoubtedly true that observation is unrivalled in enabling researchers to immerse themselves in the research environment and correlatively in drawing the reader into the world of researchers and researched. For these reasons observation is fundamental to the processes of ethnographic methods and is also often associated with the grounded theory approach made famous by Glaser and Strauss (1967). The increasing use of first-person narrative in research reports and theses has also enabled observation to come to the fore in both undergraduate and postgraduate research. Not too many years ago such methods of reporting and writing up would have been frowned upon by many in the academic community but such responses are now, thankfully, rare. If you are researching the complex social setting of the classroom, the lecture theatre, or staffroom you will need to consider whether observation should form part of your approach.

Observation can enable you to gather data on a range of settings, including the physical setting (that is, the physical environment of the organization), the human setting (the way people are organized, the numbers and types of people that are employed), the interactional setting (the forms of interactions

Table 8.1   Forms of observation (adapted from Burton et al., 2008)

Form of observation	Key features
Highly structured	The researcher works out exactly what features they are looking for prior to commencing observation. Observation categories will have been worked out and structured observational tools will have been developed to record data. Observation will be highly systematic and methods of analysis are likely to be statistical.
Semi-structured	The researcher will have worked out the main issues that they wish to explore and so will have a clear conception of what it is they wish to observe. The observational tool used to record data will also be worked out in advance, but is likely to allow note-taking rather than highly structured responses. Observation will be semi-systematic and methods of analysis are likely to be qualitative, although some basic numeric analysis may be undertaken.
Unstructured	The researcher will only have a generalized conception of what is to be observed, probably relating to an overall research theme or issue. The research tools for recording data are likely to be unstructured and also likely to take the form of notes. Methods of analysis will be qualitative.

and exchanges that are taking place and the ways they are planned), and the programme setting (such as resources, teaching, or other professional styles or approaches) (Morrison, 1993: 80).

Observation can take a variety of forms (Cohen, Manion and Morrison, 2000: 305) which are listed in Table 8.1. Robson (1993: 316–319) distinguishes between the *complete participant*, where the observer actually conceals that they are a researcher in order to become a full member of a group; the *participant as observer*, where the researcher makes clear that they are observing the situation from the start but still tries to establish close relationships with the group; the *marginal participant*, where the researcher adopts a largely passive role and merely watches what is going on, but is nonetheless a participant in the group; and the *observer-as-participant*, where the researcher takes no part in the activity whatsoever, although their role is known throughout. Such a continuum will reflect the nature of the research being carried out, and will almost certainly imply whether the researcher wishes to operate within the interpretive or positivist paradigms with consonant effects on methods of analysis. For instance, the complete participant is most likely to be engaged in some form of highly ethnographic process whereby the researcher wishes to be immersed fully within a particular culture. At the other extreme, the observer-as-participant is far more likely to be interested in a scientific or semi-scientific approach that will enable appropriate statistical procedures to be applied to the data that are gathered.

In choosing which type of observation to undertake you will need to reflect on a variety of variables in order to make a decision, and these will include your research aims and which method is most likely to fulfil them, your background training and whether it predisposes you to qualitative or quantitative approaches, the access you are likely to be able gain to the group, and even your ethical standpoint with regard to informing those under observation of your intentions. For these reasons you must ask yourself what problems you might encounter if you try to employ observation in your current (or a related) work setting, and what sort of sensitivities you would need to deal with, since observation that is not planned well and agreed in advance by those who are to be observed can be obtrusive at best and unethical at worst.

Research tools and methods of recording data

The flexibility of the observational method means that an extremely wide variety of data-recording approaches may be employed. The nature of such tools will depend in the original aims of the research project and the intended research paradigm or paradigms that you intend to operate within. Crucially, your research tool must be structured in such a way as to enable the methods of analysis you intend to employ. For this reason your recording methods will vary widely according to your skills, training and personal predilections. Indeed observation is an area of research which enables the widest set of approaches of almost any of the many methods available to researchers. Even a general research text such as Cohen et al. (2000: 311–313) lists two detailed pages of methods of recording, whilst, similarly, Sarantakos (1998: 214–217) offers almost three pages on the topic. These include approaches such as:

- making quick jottings of key words or the use of symbols;
- taking detailed notes or field notes which may cover pre-determined themes or be in response to events as they unfold;
- creating pen portraits of participants;
- describing events, behaviour or activities;
- constructing 'chronologs' describing events or episodes along with their time of occurrence, or recording observations at predetermined times;
- making context maps, sketches, or other non-verbal representations;
- using rating scales, checklists or taxonomies;
- constructing sociometric diagrams that indicate relationships between people, or show key shifts in control such as changing speakers in a staff meeting.

At its simplest, recording observations may take place via brief notes in a diary recording phenomena as they occur. Some researchers will employ specially constructed diaries for this purpose which may be put together in such a way as to give some form of structure to the observation, while others will merely use notes and footnotes in general diaries (although we would expect that such an ad hoc approach would form just one element in a more carefully constructed approach). The paramount concern here is that important events or occurrences are captured and that the chronology is noted so that the evolution of any patterns can be determined.

Contemporaneous diary writing will give you an opportunity to record observations in an extremely rich form that will be especially useful in the more reflexive types of research. The advent of accountability activities such as appraisal and performance management has increased the prevalence of

Curriculum development observation research project
Name of observer: Individual observed: Group observed: Date: Time: Focus of lesson:
Quality of teaching and learning and of the curriculum:
Student attitudes, values and personal development:
Classroom management:
General observations:

Figure 8.1 Curriculum development observation schedule

observation activities as a normal part of institutional life. For this reason, researchers will frequently adopt an observation schedule that enables structured observation according to key themes in a manner which mirrors those used in many inspection regimes. Figure 8.1 offers an example of such an observational tool that focuses on curriculum development and might be employed by a researcher interested in the efficacy of certain curricula approaches, innovations, or action research activities. A simple form such as this should contain key information like the names of the observer and observed, as well as the date and time, and provide a matrix for note-taking against pre-determined themes that relate to the research aims.

Critical event analysis	
Critical event number: Group/class: Date: Focus of event:	Name of teacher: Time:
What precipitated the event:	
What took place:	
Outcomes:	
Notes on interviews with participants:	

Figure 8.2 Critical event analysis schedule

A modified version of such a schedule is suitable for critical incident/critical event observation. Such events or occurrences are deemed to be especially important since they may typify or illuminate a particular feature of organizational culture or social interaction. Such approaches are most often employed by those who are interested in behaviour management, student integration problems, or issues relating to the student-student, client-client, or staff-client interface. Figure 8.2 shows an example of a critical event analysis schedule where particularly significant occurrences, as defined in a research protocol, can be recorded.

Some academic commentators, such as Bryman (2004), emphasize a more systematic approach to observation, with a concomitant requirement for an observation schedule that incorporates a clear focus and a simple system of recording that takes account of subsequent systems of coding of data and shows due consideration for reliability and validity (Bryman, 2004: 169–170). Such approaches will enable highly structured methods that may employ dia-critical marks or other symbols to record events in a manner which will be familiar to those trained in psychology. For instance, Figure 8.3 provides an apparently simple representation of how much time off task individuals in a group of 10 children spent during a ten-minute period of observation. The chart gives a very straightforward numeric representation of the number of occasions when children failed to pay attention to their work. At first sight it may seem to be useful in providing a fairly precise indication of which children within the group were attentive and which were not. However, such a schematic representation might give rise to a series of other important questions. For instance, children 1 and 5 seem to be off-task for the greatest amount of time during the fifteen minutes of observation, but does the chart give a hint as to why they were off task? Is child 3 instigating an interaction that may cause a breakdown in concentration? Why is child 7 apparently attentive until the final minutes of the period of observation? Has she, for instance, completed all the work given to her and become bored? And why does child 9 appear to be on-task for most of the period but have brief periods when she is off-task and then, apparently, goes back to work? Such questions are tantalising and cannot be answered by such a chart in isolation. They need to be followed up by further observation which focuses on the types or forms of interaction of only one or two individuals at a time in a way that will allow for much more detailed qualitative analysis. This is not to say that such an observation chart is not of value in itself. In its own right it will provide clear and precise indications of the length of time that a particular individual or an entire group of children is undertaking a particular task, and this can be analyzed through the use of simple statistical techniques in a way that may inform researchers about the efficacy and interest levels of particular curricula approaches or pieces of work. This technique could then be employed as a pre- and post-test to see whether some change in the materials or pedagogic technique would encourage engagement by pupils, or it could perhaps be used as one amongst a variety of methods to investigate complex sets of relationships amongst children.

	Time in one-minute intervals														
	1	2	3	4	5	6	7	8	9	10	11	12	13	14	15
1. Joanne		X	X	X				X	X	X	X				
2. Diane															
3. Neil	X						X	X							
4. Chris			X											X	X
5. Freddie		X	X	X	X	X	X								
6. Jane															
7. Pat												X	X	X	X
8. Richard															
9. Hattie						X					X				
10. Paul									X	X	X				

Name of child (row axis label)

X indicates time off task

Figure 8.3 Chart of time off task over a fifteen minute period

Minor modifications to such a chart can enable it to be used for very different purposes. So instead of measuring 'negative' activities such as time off task, the observations could focus on seeing the extent to which young children were socializing and cooperating in their work. See Figure 8.4 below.

In using such a schedule you would need to ask what key features of an observation schedule would be relevant to your professional context, and whether that schedule was susceptible to quantitative or qualitative data analysis or both. Such schedules can be infinitely flexible and even minor changes can mean that more, or more relevant, data can be gathered which will add great richness to your research project. For instance, Figure 8.4 focuses on the level of socialization or interaction of pupils or students and, in this case, also allows for note-taking to gather richer data on the reasons for the level of engagement.

	Socialization/interaction level			
	High	*Medium*	*Low*	*Notes*
10.00				
10.05				
10.10				
10.15				
10.20				
10.25				
10.30				

Time in 5 minutes (row axis label)

Figure 8.4 Socialization/interaction level

Methods of analysis for observational data

The forms of observation that are susceptible to qualitative analysis may be examined either by the use of 'traditional' methods of data interrogation or the increasing number of electronic data analysis packages. Any decision you make on whether to employ electronic means will be both individual and pragmatic. Some experienced researchers will continue to use manual means even if they have the skills to employ electronic approaches, and they will do this because they wish to remain in close personal contact with the data; others will regularly use electronic means even when exploring comparatively small amounts of material. However, a general rule is that small-scale pieces of research that have elicited comparatively little qualitative data may not be worth the time and effort of coming to grips with the complexities of electronic approaches unless learning such techniques is itself a goal of the researcher. Note that whether you are using electronic or manual means the essence of qualitative analysis remains the same: you must look for key commonalities within the data that indicate linkages, illuminate research questions, or point to emerging themes within the data. This process will be facilitated by your close reading of the material that has been derived from observation, and where this is in the form of notes, diary entries or other means of recording where speech may be involved, you will need to allocate key phrases, utterances or incidents to pre-determined or emergent themes or nodes. This might follow a straightforward path where you will transcribe original notes and primary data, and then follow this by a close reading of the material: during this you will need to highlight the main concepts, either manually or electronically, and categorize and order the resulting material. A simple stem-and-branch analysis would include the creation of key themes from original research objectives, and these might then form the basis for a series of matrices with emergent sub-themes.

Wragg (1999) cautioned those who were untrained in statistical approaches to consult a statistician rather than misuse a procedure. However, he suggested also that the following techniques are the most common and most appropriate ways for analyzing observational data through statistical methods:

Relationships between measures – used to calculate the relationship between two measures, such as the amount of misbehaviour and number of pupils applying themselves to a task.

Comparing groups – dependant on the type of measure involved. If a frequency count has been taken a chi square may be appropriate, but other techniques such as a t-test, Mann-Whitney U, or Kruskal-Wallis analysis may be appropriate.

Measuring change – especially useful in calculating 'value-added', and thus for comparing the progress of unmatched groups.

Predicting – multiple regression analysis.

Reducing complexity – factor analysis or cluster analysis.
Aggregating findings – used to put together findings from several different pieces of observational research. Most commonly associated with 'meta-analysis'(Wragg, 1999: 123–127).

A chapter on observation is not the place for a detailed outline of either qualitative or statistical techniques of analysis, but there are a range of excellent texts providing detailed instructions on where and how to apply such approaches that are accessible to the non-specialist. If you are interested in qualitative approaches you might like to examine the work of Miles and Huberman (1994) or Silverman (2004). If you are seeking guidance on quantitative approaches we would recommend Solomon and Winch (1994); Clegg (1994); Cohen and Holliday (1996); or Bryman and Cramer (1997).

Ethics and observational methods

It is easy to overlook ethical issues when employing observational techniques since observational methods do not employ intervention and may be perceived to be part of 'normal professional duties'. Nonetheless, as noted earlier, observation may be employed as a result of critical incidents or it may act as the precursor to intervention as part of an action research cycle. Even when disassociated from intervention the act of observation is itself a matter of extreme sensitivity, since it will involve at least an element of judgement-making that may be deemed too sensitive within the social context of the workplace. For instance, when observing a classroom, judgements may be made about the quality of teaching and learning, thus potentially impugning the professional competence of the colleague observed or students' abilities. Moreover, any observation of child subjects will always contain potential problems since child protection issues will be paramount. Additionally, it is crucial we recognize and acknowledge that observation as part of research processes should never be confused with observation for accountability or other managerial processes. This should form part of the 'contract' between the observer and the observed so there should be no doubt that data gathered in the process of research observation will be used solely for the purposes of the research project and will not be employed as part of competence or capability procedures.

Whether or not to intervene when undertaking observation

The subject of whether or not to intervene during the process of observation is a vexed one, and is not infrequently the subject of lively discussion and conjecture amongst academic colleagues involved in such data-gathering processes. Of course there are no real issues if a researcher has chosen to undertake the role of 'participant observer' since intervention, discussion and engagement form part of the research process. The situation is, however, far more complex for the non-participant observer who has determined to operate without taking part in the activity that is the focus of the observation. The nub of the issue usually revolves around when and whether it is appropriate to interject if as observers we see something occur, or about to occur, that is inappropriate or dangerous. There are several disadvantages to such an intervention, including the fact that we will inevitably cease to function as researchers because we will ourselves become part of the activity under scrutiny. Furthermore, any such intervention may be very distressing to those being observed since it may be seen to imply some lack of ability by those in charge of the activity. As researchers we will all face such a situation at some time during the process of observational research, and we will need to make a professional decision about whether or not to intercede based on the circumstances. In general, our decision will focus on whether there is likelihood of injury, either physical or emotional, to the subjects.

Summary ☐

Observation is one of the most powerful and most overlooked of research approaches. Frequently those undertaking research projects in the social sciences will have finely honed skills in observation that will have accrued after years of training and professional practice, and within which the scrutiny of colleagues and, most importantly, clients, pupils or students, will form an integral part of their role. The use of observation does not predetermine or even imply the dominant research tradition the researcher intends to work within, since data gathered using such methods can be employed as part of either a positivist or interpretive approach to data interrogation. Such decisions about paradigmatic approaches will, however, be inherent in the nature of the actual research tools developed, since only certain forms of observational recording will be susceptible to qualitative or quantitative approaches. However, some forms of data-gathering will be susceptible to both quantitative and qualitative methods or, even more commonly, will enable an interaction between methods. Alternatively, one research tool that employs observation may be employed as the concomitant of another element within a blended approach.

Researchers employing observational techniques must be extremely sensitive to ethical considerations as the process of observation may be easily be confused with some form of onerous surveillance by the subject or subjects of observation. It is essential that all those who are involved in the research process are completely clear about how the data derived from such methods will be employed, and aware that there will be no question that such material will be used for other purposes such as appraisal or performance management.

Despite such complexities and challenges, observation can be one of the most rewarding of research approaches. Although observation may act as, and indeed has formed, the main research tool for major, funded research studies, it can also be a particularly relevant method for small-scale research by practitioner researchers.

Further reading

DeWalt, K.M. and DeWalt, B.R. (2001) *Participant Observation: A Guide for Fieldworkers.* London: Altamira.

Fine, G.A. and Sandstrom, K.L. (1998) *Knowing Children: Participant Observation with Minors (Qualitative Research Methods).* London: Sage.

Hopkins, D. (2007) *A Teacher's Guide to Classroom Research.* Milton Keynes: Open University Press.

Montgomery, D. (2002) *Helping Teachers Develop Through Classroom Observation.* London: David Fulton.

Rodriguez, N.M. and Ryave, A.L. (2002) *Systematic Self-Observation: A Method for Researching the Hidden and Elusive Features of Everyday Social Life (Qualitative Research Methods).* London: Sage.

Sharman, C., Vennis, D. and Cross, W. (1995) *Observing Children: A Practical Guide (Cassell Studies in Pastoral Care and Personal and Social Education).* London: Continuum.

9

Documentary Analysis

Aims

The use of documentary analysis often appears in the design section of theses and dissertations. Its use may be as a single method, but far more frequently it is utilized alongside other methods in a case study context. Students will generally offer some details on what documents have been analyzed, some details on how the analysis has been undertaken, the place of documentary analysis in the overall research design, and finally, some indication of how the findings from the documentary analysis informed the overall findings of the larger study. Documentary analysis spans a continuum from the straightforward use of documents to help confirm a particular point to a more complex categorization and coding studies intended to seek meaning and intention within texts. Documents can be used as items of evidence within a larger evidential base or form the subject of the research in their own right. A further use of documents is in the creation of the critical literature review to provide a background to the research project, and inform the contextual or theoretical base to be adopted and used in discussing the findings. In this chapter we offer coverage of how to address such a critical literature review. We also include content which aims to inform you about the various kinds of document available, how they may be accessed, and how some of the more complex textual, content and discourse analyzes undertaken by researchers have been used to advance their studies. We also aim to convey a logical pathway to undertaking documentary analysis, along with some thoughts on associated ethical, sampling and reliability issues. Overall we hope to provide you with a stepping stone towards this important method within the field of leadership research. By the end of this chapter you should be able to:

- perceive the importance of documents in leadership research;
- understand what documents are and how they can be accessed;
- see how the literature review can best be organized to acquire and store
  relevant documents;
- understand the main principles and methods of analyzing documents.

The importance of documents in leadership research

Leadership research will inevitably require you to engage in a good deal of reading of academic papers, books, internet sites, and other forms of recorded material pertinent to the research at hand. Such reading can inform you about the antecedents of a particular study, broaden your perspectives, reveal gaps in your current knowledge base, and help legitimize arguments. Selected documents may become part of the evidence base you use to advance an argument and draw conclusions or, as mentioned above, selected documents may themselves become the subject of your research focus. Documents pertaining to education are numerous and analyzing these demands a method of qualitative inquiry which can often be used alongside the various other methods available to leadership researchers. For example, documentary analysis is often chosen as one of the methods used in case study research as it allows researchers to interpret what is being said as well as how it is being said, and offer an explanation.

Analyzing documents may give rise to better or new understandings about the historical backdrop to events, the social and political agendas prevailing at the time, the intentions of documents and even the authors themselves. To undertake analysis you will have to interrogate the document and seek answers. Scott (1996) suggests that documents may be questioned to yield evidence about their authenticity, credibility, representativeness and meaning. All of these would be important if you were attempting to describe, interpret and explain, as accurately as possible, past events to those who would access your research. Documents are recordings of events and perceptions at a particular time that are set within and produced against a backdrop of the prevailing cultural, socio-economic, political and policy environment. Note that the content and style of documents may well be influenced by their temporal context and may even be critical of prevailing regimes at the time of their production. For example, the recent introduction of academy schools in England needs to be understood in terms of current and prevailing political, economic and social drivers. Indeed critical analysis of documents associated with this change has contributed to a robust political and academic debate about the values, ownership and social justice of education in England in the early twenty first century.

To help illustrate the analysis of documents where the documents themselves are the subject of the research, we would point you towards work by Winograd (2011) who undertook an exploratory study of racism in a genre of children's literature. This researcher analyzed the text of eight popular biographies of professional football players. Sentences within the text were coded using the guidance of key questions such as, 'How is the text describing the player? How do I interpret the explicit and implicit intent of the authors in their descriptions of the players? (2011: 337). From this coding a set of categories could be

constructed to help explicate deeper insights, such as showing power relationships and an individualistic stance towards achievement (ibid.: 338). Whether
used in a literature review to frame and advance a particular study, or as an
essential part of an evidence base, or as the subjects of research themselves, it
is worthwhile remembering that documents are an essential source of information in leadership research.

What are documents and how are they accessed?

The term 'document' includes an impressive array of items that you may draw
upon. Your list might include sources such as books, journals, government
publications, newspapers, prospectuses, reports and policies from individual
organizations, letters, diaries, census records, photographs, websites, audio
and video recordings, models and other physical items. For example, drawing
on photographs of schools and classrooms, Grosvenor et al. (2004) provided
a fascinating debate to bring together the historian and the photographer.
They chose to read the photograph not only as an image but also as a text,
and included photographs as items that were firmly within the domain of
documentary analysis. Adopting a different focus, Goodman and Grosvenor
(2009) employed a thematic analysis of journal contents and concluded that
with respect to the history of education there was a growing focus on the
education of women and girls and the activities of women educators, and also
a readiness on the part of educational researchers who were not historians of
education to adopt an historical dimension to their work. In an American
setting, Brantlinger (2011) undertook a comparative textual analysis of three
secondary geometry texts to examine how the incorporation of critical or
political themes into the required secondary mathematics curriculum trans-
formed this curriculum, basing his comparative textual analysis on an analytic framework developed by Dowling (1998). In a recent study to investigate
how can we enhance the enjoyment of secondary school from the point of
view of students, Gorard and See (2011) used documentary analysis, official
statistics, interviews and surveys. In this case, documents such as the organization's strategic plans, achievement, retention and progression data, pro-
spectus, policy and information on advice and guidance, staff numbers/
structure and curriculum range were collected from each of the participating
educational organizations.

In undertaking documentary analysis sampling needs to be taken into
account. Denscombe (2003: 220) reminds us that a single document may not be
representative of its type. A leadership researcher may be given documents by a
school, but what selection procedures have the school applied? Do they convey
the real story or complexity? Will the research be limited by restricted access to
documents? Again, as with the application of other research methods, access
and sampling need to be considered at the design stage of a research project.

Similarly, the provenance and validity of documents used in research are important. In some cases, reports of the outcomes of paid evaluations have been considered to be potentially biased in the view of the commissioner or the benefactor of the research. This is, of course, not always the case. Wallace and Poulson (2003) offer insights into the critical analysis of individual research items promoting questions concerning, for example, the depth of the evidence that conclusions are based upon and the likely trustworthiness of the findings based upon the design employed. Quality, authenticity, credibility and trustworthiness should be at the forefront of your thinking in the selection process. As with all other methods of research, it is ethically necessary (see BERA, 2011) that you request and obtain permission to access and analyze documents from an institution. Your awareness of maintaining strict ethical standards at all times is thus very important. For example, individuals may be named in selected documents or items may be sensitive in some other way. If you are employed in the particular institution where the required documents reside and are therefore relatively easy to obtain, then your seeking permission still pertains as such documents may be confidential or in some cases commercially sensitive.

However, do remember that many documents exist in the public domain and can therefore be accessed by anyone (for example, school inspection data, items in libraries and other collections, and items on websites such as that for the National College for School Leadership in England). You can also seek out and access documentary items using electronic databases such as the British Education Index and internet sources such as Google Scholar. These can add new insights to your research projects. In summary, documentary analysis is generally thought of as a type of qualitative analysis which relies on the collection of documents, subsequent analysis of the contents to identify their significant features, and finally, the drawing of resultant conclusions from that analysis. In the next section of the chapter we will focus on a critical literature review as an essential item in research activity. Indeed some critical literature reviews constitute whole papers in their own right, and serve to inform co-workers of the current research and thinking in the leadership field or in research design and methods.

The relationship between documentary analysis and the literature review

In Chapter 4 of this text we discussed some of the main issues in creating a critical literature review as a means to explore the antecedents of a study and establish gaps in the available knowledge base, inform researchers about the relevant tenets to emerge from the review, aid in the formulation of studies and questions, and foster the development of the argument that will appear in the final report for dissemination. As we argued earlier, the literature review is an integral part of the research and should be structured around the research questions: hence it must be contained and focused. It is vital that you are certain about the purposes of the literature review, especially in your thesis or dissertation work. Your main purpose should be to apply a questioning and critical approach to the literature in order to further inform the focus of your research and enable a progressively focused clarity of thought: this will allow your literature review to encompass your key issues and themes, as well as establish a conceptual or theoretical framework that will help you analyze your findings and address the final research questions.

We have also emphasized that searching the literature should be carried in a systematic way, and it is only by carrying out such a review that you can be confident that all (or at least most) of the documents that are relevant to the study which are extant in the literature can be acquired and subsequently analyzed. A search strategy for the appropriate documents might include the following:

- Recent books and theses.
- Selected journals.
- Conference papers.
- Electronic services such as the British Education Index which can be interrogated using key words and key authors.
- Websites such as that for the National College for School Leadership.
- Search engines such as Google Scholar.

The documents you discover may be presented in the same way as we have suggested for the overall literature and indeed, for most of the time you will deal with these in the same way as the overall literature search. The documents may, therefore, be stored in chronological order to illustrate how thinking or policy has changed over time, or on a thematic basis, taking key issues/themes from the publications included and discussing these one at a time. In some cases you will be able to manage the publications so that they fall neatly into a number of quite different areas (for example, current models of leadership, leadership for diversity and leadership for learning). Note that this kind of review is sometimes referred to as a narrative review or perhaps an expert commentary.

We have stated that a review of the literature aims to critically analyze existing material pertinent to the subject and context of the research at hand. It enables the creation of a coherent story, builds arguments pertaining to the research, and offers a theoretical framework in which the research will take place. The antecedents of any study are crucial for informing and helping you analyze the research and the findings that emerge from it: they can also enable the focus of the research to be sharpened. They show what is known about the area of the research and importantly they show what is *not* known. A range of material can be accessed in addition to the standard texts or journal articles, and this may reflect theory, research, policy, and practice in a systematic way, as well as include materials from government and its agencies, papers and reports from educational organizations, academic publications, practitioner publications, internet sources and textbooks. As previously mentioned, the quality of the material can vary and some of it might have a focus driven by a particular ideology or sponsor. Much however will be of high quality and credible, in that it is based on a true, sufficient, and unbiased investigation.

Note that a difference exists here with respect to primary and secondary sources. A primary source may be, for example, government statistics or a technical report, and could offer information which has not been analyzed or synthesized according to another researcher's perspective. A secondary source, in contrast, would be a textbook which has taken the work of others and perhaps primary sources and reworked a synthesis of these in order to offer a summarized perspective. A review which is focused, structured, informative and balanced will be most useful. Do remember though that a critical approach to reading the material is called for, meaning that blindly accepting all that is written is perhaps not the best approach. The rigour and quality of the information, the interpretation you give this, the level of agreement or disagreement between authors, and taking the view that alternative explanations may be possible, are all part of such a critical approach. In arriving at a review which gives an account of the current state of knowledge pertaining to the intended research, it is good practice to summarize the key issues and themes to emerge from the review. What has been learnt? What conceptual framework should be brought forward to help analyze findings from the subsequent research work? And finally, does the learning which has taken place warrant a change in focus for the intended research? There are many texts which will inform you on how to systematically search the literature and read it critically. For example, Hart (1998), Wallace and Poulson (2003), Campbell, McNamara and Gilroy (2004) and Thomas (2009), all have value in this respect. Above all, it will be your clarity of thinking and progressive focusing at this stage that will enable you to produce a research design that is fit for purpose.

Here is a series of working steps that could help you create a critical review of the documents:

1. Select the topic.
2. Define the terminology.
3. Decide on the search parameters, terms and limitations.
4. Select the sources.
5. Avoid presenting work author by author or article by article.
6. Identify any issues, gaps, consensus and dissonance.
7. Make a coherent pattern reflecting the themes and/or chronology.
8. Analyze rather than over-rely on description.
9. Use quotes to establish or illustrate points as required.
10. Summarize the review to show a conceptual framework.

11. Ask yourself if what you have learned would result in an amendment to your original research questions?
12. Note that whatever you cite must appear in a reference list at the end of your work.

A vast number of publications have become available in the leadership field of study over recent years. This clearly makes searching for material more difficult, and can complicate the selection of documents when unbiased and good quality information is needed within a limited time-frame. As noted in Chapter 4, nationally since 1993, the EPPI Centre based at the Institute of Education in London has been at the forefront of undertaking systematic reviews and developing review methods in social science and public policy. The Centre aims to make reliable research findings available to those who need them. In summary, this kind of systematic review can identify all relevant published (and unpublished) evidence and select which evidence should be included in a particular review. The quality of these items can be assessed according to the desired criteria and synthesized in an unbiased way. The final product is aimed at presenting a rigorous, balanced and impartial report. In many ways, these large systematic reviews mirror the processes needed to secure the shorter and focused reviews that are typically found in leadership articles, theses, and dissertations.

Doing documentary analysis

Documentary analysis may be applied to individual documents or collections of documents, thereby making the documents(s) themselves the focus of research. In some kinds of historical research, documentary analysis can also be used for identifying authorship. The outcomes of such analysis may be utilized as evidence or as part of the evidence in a research study. Typically the flow of activities you would need to undertake would be:

1. Establish the focus of the research.
2. Identify the documents to be analyzed and sample appropriately.
3. Decide on the unit of analysis (e.g. a words, phrases or sentences).
4. Decide on the categories you wish to use for the analysis (these identify key issues within the research and are set to be mutually exclusive).
5. Code the categories (emergent from the text or *a priori* using a chosen theoretical base).
6. Test the coding on samples of text to ensure reliability.
7. Run the analysis (by hand, or by using computer programs to assist in the analysis of multiple documents).

Morris and Ecclesfield (2011) have recently developed a new, computer-aided technique for qualitative document analysis and offered illustrative examples.

This technique may have benefits when the research is required to deal with large amounts of text. Using available technology, Gill and Griffin (2010) advocate the use of Tag clouds, a feature of the World Wide Web, in the rapid analysis of textual data to reveal textual messages in a pictorial form. Tag clouds enable dominant words to be identified in a ready visual form and can therefore make prominent messages stand out for readers. Working in a medical context, Gill and Griffin argue that the use of tag clouds can enable a reader to see common terms or emphases in a text and in turn conclude that tag clouds are useful for policy researchers to reduce textual data and identify embedded discourses.

Denscombe (2003) uses the term 'content analysis' to convey the idea that it is an analysis of the contents of documents that is taking place and content categories are being established. Such an analysis may also be used for quantifying the contents of a text. For example, in a paper concerned with the assessment of school anti-bullying policies, Smith et al. (2008) undertook a content analysis of 142 school anti-bullying policies. A 31-item scoring scheme was devised to assess policy. The items acted as a coding scheme which could be applied and used to score each policy with respect to the items identified by the researchers. The findings showed a great range of scores for the adequacy of school anti-bullying policies. They also found that adequacy or inadequacy was not related to the length of the policy document. Bos and Tarnai (1999) give an overview of the development of empirical content analysis. The development of a category scheme is the central objective of content analysis and after this the distribution of codes to the text can begin. In short, content analysis can be used as a systematic way to analyze trends and patterns in documents. It is a powerful data-reduction technique enabling the reduction of many words into content categories based upon coding. It depends upon clear definitions of categories and the creation of mutually exclusive categories. As mentioned in Chapter 3 of this book, in documentary analysis reliability may be open to questions based upon issues pertaining to text coding. Consistency in understanding the meaning of words, in coding rules and in category rules is required, and this will help secure greater reliability. A high degree of reproducibility, either by a single coder or by different coders using the same text, will indicate a good level of reliability. Triangulation may also be used to increase validity, for example, by utilizing multiple sources of data, methods or researchers. The power of content analysis relates to coding and categorizing data. Codes may emerge following examination of the data, or alternatively these may be established before the document is examined based upon a theoretical stance that is drawn from the existing literature.

Using a textual analysis Kuenssberg (2011) has investigated the current mission statements of 20 Scottish universities to reveal their aims and priorities. The study identifies the main themes present in the university mission statements and compares the vocabulary used with recent government policy documents. The findings show much similarity between the mission statements but also identify some surprising omissions, and suggest that our understanding of the prevailing political context may be related to the way the universities present themselves. Overall, the method adopted consists of a content analysis, a keyword analysis, and finally a comparison of keywords to recent Scottish policy documents. The study concludes that there is a tendency for mission statements to feedback to politicians the objectives set for the universities, as shown by the congruence of the mission statement's language with current government policy documents. The statements also reflect self-promotion and claim excellence in a strongly competitive higher education marketplace.

Also set in a higher education context, Borg and Deane (2011) offer a model for analyzing the changes in student writing as a result of individualized writing instruction. The textual analysis provided focuses on five essential items of writing mastery that need to be achieved by students in their first year of study. These items are: fulfilment of the assignment brief; information structure; sentence-level analysis; vocabulary analysis; and proof-reading errors. Although the long-term effects of writing support interventions are unknown, Borg and Deane argue that some measure of the effectiveness of interventions is now possible by employing this textual analysis approach, and additionally, that a basis for possible future improvements to interventions has been established. As an additional illustration of how text content may be analyzed we draw on the work of Vanstone and Kinsella (2010), who focused on metaphors in a study to examine whether the prenatal screening educational materials available to Canadian women were consistent with aims to be nondirective, promote choice, and be respectful of the needs and quality of life of people with disabilities. A metaphoric textual analysis was employed as it was understood that metaphoric language may help in shaping our understanding of the world. Implicit messages in the educational materials were sought and Vanstone and Kinsella employed metaphoric textual analysis to foster critical reflection on the implicit and ideological stances that could be embedded within the metaphors used in the text (2010: 456). They found some success with this method.

The term 'discourse analysis' is also used to convey the activity of coding text in order to discover patterns within it. Robson (1993) argues that language potentially holds a key in understanding human functioning by understanding what is said and how it is said. Cohen et al. (2003) suggest that in discourse analysis the coding of the text by a researcher, leading to the discovery of patterns in the discourse, can be followed by a further examination of the text to reveal intentions within it so as to come closer to a true interpretation of what the discourse conveys within its context. In a recent paper, Barker and Rossi (2011) argue that discourse analysis could be used to better understand the ways teachers make sense of what they do.

Discourse analysis holds the potential to generate new ways of understanding teachers' explanatory frameworks. Barker and Rossi contend that all concepts are embedded within a personal and communal set of assumptions, and that an examination of teachers' repertoires can offer insights into the meanings teachers bring to bear in their teaching. In summary, analyzing the content of documents is not just simply a word frequency counting exercise as word frequency may or may not be related to author intention, and whilst documentary analysis can be far more complicated than this, it represents a worthwhile and exacting method, one that is worthy of consideration by leadership researchers given its appropriateness to the focus of their research.

Summary ☐

The research method of documentary analysis can be seen as spanning a range of possible activities, from the straightforward use of documents to help confirm or extend particular points within an argument, to complex studies intended to seek out meaning and author intention within selected texts. Documents can constitute items of evidence within a larger evidential base or form the subject of a research investigation in their own right. In this chapter we included a consideration of the use of documents in undertaking the familiar activity of a critical literature review: this is used to provide information about the antecedents of studies, and in informing the contextual or theoretical base to be adopted and used to discuss emergent research findings. Documentary analysis in the form of textual or content analysis is presented as being much more than counting the occurrence of words or phrases in a text. Rather, it is addressed as a systematic categorization and coding of text offering challenges and opportunities to the leadership researcher as they seek patterns and meaning within that text. We also included the analysis of discourse which may be available as a written recording, but of course, does refer to items of language and the spoken word. It is included here as it too depends upon a skilful coding of items to enable the analysis to take place. In a more straightforward way, and perhaps as part of a case study investigation, the inclusion of documents as part of the evidential base will be more familiar to many leadership researchers. For example, in seeking to research the leadership of communities of practice within schools, a leadership researcher may wish to include and examine school policies, professional development records, mission statements, and items such as the minutes of school council meetings. Overall, documentary analysis carries many advantages and it and its use is well established in the form of the critical literature review. It can also help in the triangulation of other evidence. At all times leadership researchers should be vigilant about gaining access to required documents and the ethics of their use, especially if these are not in the general public domain. Vigilance is also required concerning the authenticity, credibility and representativeness of chosen documents, unless, of course, the intention is to analyze documents with a view to seeking the biases they may contain. Documents are of their time and context and thus can provide fascinating insights for researchers within the field.

Further reading

Avery, H. (2010) *Doing a Literature Review in Health and Social Care: A Practical Guide* (2nd edition). Maidenhead: Open University Press.

Denscombe, M. (2010) *The Good Research Guide* (4th edition). Maidenhead: Open University Press.

Hart, C. (1998) *Doing a Literature Review: Releasing the Social Science Research Imagination.* London: Sage.

McCulloch, G. (2004) *Documentary Research: In Education, History and the Social Sciences.* London: Routledge.

Rapley, T. (2008) *Doing Conversation, Discourse and Document Analysis* (Qualitative Research Kit). London: Sage.

Wallace, M. and Poulson, L. (2003) *Learning to Read Critically in Educational Leadership and Management.* London: Sage.

10

Action Research and Practitioner Inquiry

Aims

Action research is a very popular approach for practitioner researchers since it has at its heart a commitment to change and innovation. This has a natural appeal for educational leaders who are, by nature, committed to improving institutional effectiveness. Action research also has many links to 'reflective practice', which is also a popular approach for enhancing the performance of educators in order to increase outcomes for learners. By the end of this chapter you should be able to:

- understand the nature of action research as an approach to research generally, and educational leadership initiatives specifically;
- recognize the strengths and weaknesses of action research and its relationship to 'reflective practice';
- construct an appropriate action research strategy suitable for the research context and the conceptual focus.

The nature of action research

Action research encourages the use of mixed methods and an objective research perspective, combined with active intervention, and therefore employs an iterative research process to steer an initiative towards a desired outcome. Each iteration is informed and directed by an analysis of the evidence gathered and consideration of the conceptual literature and relevant published research findings. For example, a school leader wishing to examine the efficacy of an approach to the professional development of colleagues may want to explore whether utilizing a particular leadership training programme has proved successful in achieving a set of defined outcomes and in the broader enhancement of institutional effectiveness. This might involve an analysis of needs, the setting of certain goals, the development and implementation of a programme of development, the

gathering of evidence about the efficacy of the programme, any adjust-
ment to the approach, further training, a further assessment of outcomes,
and so on.

Practitioner action research is commonly associated with the concept of
'reflective practice' (Schön, 1983; 1987), a process within which reflection
can be triggered by the recognition that in some respects a situation is in
need of special attention (Eraut, 1994:144). Most teachers engage in this
process regularly in their day-to-day practice when they reflect on how a
particular group of pupils is responding to a new teaching approach, learning strategy or resource, and whether this new idea requires further
modification, or if it should be retained or abandoned. Sometimes, such
reflection manifests itself in reflective dialogues and may even provoke
action within a department or across the whole institution. Although
teacher reflection is often followed by action, and that action by reflection,
the generation of so-called evidence is often anecdotal and derived from ad
hoc experiences. As with any other form of research, practitioner action
research needs to satisfy a set of quality criteria by ensuring that the process
reflects a rigorous and systematic approach. As such it needs to go beyond
practice with a focus on knowledge that informs action rather than just the
action itself and is concerned with practitioners' values, beliefs and motives
and how these influence them in their actions (McNiff, Lomaz and
Whitehead, 1996). The action cycle starts with an issue or a problem that
has been identified in a certain situation (in the classroom or the institution
as a whole) that is in need of resolving through an intervention programme, a new strategy, or the implementation of a new framework, policy
or procedure. Practitioner action research is thus 'insider' research which
can provide teachers with a framework for enquiry into their professional
practices, enabling them to engage in critical reflection about issues related
to their own and other practice settings in a systematic manner.

Practitioner-based action research can be conducted at different levels of
critical engagement reflecting a technical, practical and emancipatory focus
(McKernan, 1991; Kemmis and McTaggart, 1992; Zuber-Skerritt, 1996). It can
be used to find solutions to technical problems, without questioning the
legitimacy of these techniques or the framework within which they are to be
applied. Where the focus of action research is practical it takes into account
social and cultural factors inherent in the setting and how these might affect
learning. For example, attendance problems may not be effectively addressed
by taking a harsher stance in terms of sanctions, and instead require action
and enquiry that incorporate a range of perspectives (pupils/students, par-
ents/carers, teachers/lecturers, children's services/learning support services).
And by allowing those at the heart of the process a voice, it would also reflect
an emancipatory agenda (Groundwater-Smith and Mockler, 2007), the core
aim of which is the empowerment of individuals and social groups that have
been marginalized and whose voices need to be heard.

Definition and key principles of action research

Action research has enjoyed a growing popularity amongst practitioners in the social sciences over recent years, since it has at its heart a commitment to improving professional practice through critical enquiry and reflection on practice (Dadds, 1995; Dadds and Hart, 2001; Campbell et al., 2004; Burton and Bartlett, 2005). Such an approach also sits well with the dominant paradigm in educational theory and practice which is that of school effectiveness and improvement (the government 'approved' approach to the leadership of schools in many nations).

The action research approach is also appealing to many in education generally, and educational leadership specifically, since its underpinning philosophy has a strong democratic dimension (Carr and Kemmis, 1986) in that it often includes 'service users' (pupils/students, parents/carers) in the research process (Beresford, 1999; Winter and Munn-Giddings, 2001) and seeks to give a voice to those who are 'culturally silenced' (Winter, 1998; Burton et al., 2010: 127). These commitments align strongly with recent developments in the theory of educational management, such as 'distributed' approaches to leadership which seek to engage a wide range of stakeholders in the development of the institution.

Action research is frequently employed to address issues arising from professional practice with the aim of constructing knowledge collaboratively in order to bring about change and improvement (Lewin, 1952; Carr and Kemmis, 1986; Elliott, 1991). It thus promotes ownership of the research process by those who will be most affected by its outcomes with the predominant aim 'to improve practice rather than to produce knowledge' (Elliott, 1991: 49). In this way action research can be seen as a form of systematic enquiry carried out by professionals into their own work activities and work environment in order to change and enhance practice (Somekh, 1995; Kemmis and McTaggart, 1997). Waterson expands on this by stating that the aim of action research is:

> to make improvements ... by working with the organisational actors in a cycle of action, data gathering, analysis, reflection and planning further action, as the researchers and the organisation work together. Praxis and research go together, each taking account of the other, and influencing the way people think about an issue. (Waterson, 2000: 495)

Figure 10.1 shows a number of key principles underpinning such research.

As the principles outlined above reveal, action research can be conducted by individuals or a group of practitioners who have identified an area in their professional practice that they consider requires further improvement. This means that those who wish to engage in this approach need to be highly sensitive to how the research may impact on their colleagues, and to how any such research project must be underpinned by the clear ethical principles

Principle 1: Action research integrates change into the research process
Action research can be distinguished from other forms of social science research by its explicit focus on action and change. Action research is usually underpinned by some form of critical theory which tries to induce change in a social setting and is committed not only to understanding the work but also changing it (Carr and Kemmis, 1986). Understanding both the objective and subjective world is part of the process but these aims of explaining and understanding serve a desire for change, renewal and improvement (Schon, 1983).

Principle 2: Action research is carried out by practitioners and focuses on their own practice
Action research is carried out by people directly concerned with the social situation where the research is located (Somekh, 2005). This is based on the principle that practice is changed best by those who are involved in the activity under scrutiny and understand the values of the situation. Thus action research is an inquiry by or with practitioners but never on practitioners (Herr and Anderson, 2005).

Principle 3: Action research locates the inquiry in an understanding of a broader context
Action research regards educational practice as social practice which is socially constructed (Kemmis, 2007). For this reason action research pays careful attention to the practitioner's understanding of practice and the social situation in which it is based with a view to improving the quality of action within it.

Principle 4: Action research involves a high level of reflexivity and sensitivity to the self
Action research involves critical self-reflection which is an active process of self-scrutiny (Heikkinen et al., 2007) since action research involves the researcher as the main focus for the research. This means that the analysis of data is always mediated by the practitioner's own background, beliefs and knowledge. This process of reflection allows practitioners to analyse and critique their own assumptions (Elliott, 2005) which may be tacit and taken-for-granted.

Principle 5: The action research perspective involves the development of publish knowledge
Action research aims to contribute to public knowledge and thus action researchers should report on their findings in order to legitimise their activities as systematic inquiry rather than simple self-reflection (Ebbutt, 1985).

Figure 10.1   Five principles of action research (adapted from Heikkinen et al., 2007; Bolat, 2013: 41–46)

inherent in the four outcomes identified by McNiff et al. (1996: 8), which include:

- personal development;
- improved professional practice;
- improvements in the institution in which one works;
- contributing to the good order of society.

McNiff and colleagues highlight the point that when we undertake action research, each of us needs to put 'I' at the centre (1996:17), and this must be accompanied with an explanation of how we are positioned in relation to the research setting and the other research participants. This has become even more important in recent years since there has been a growing emphasis on the importance of children's voice in school improvement, and so action research increasingly involves the participation of pupils in 'participatory action research' (PAR) which has as its primary aim, the transformation of situations and structures in an egalitarian manner (Gray, 2004: 375). This not only adds great depth to the approach but also inevitably leads to an even greater requirement for care in how the research is conducted and in the application of the highest ethical standards.

The action research process

As we have already noted, action research is primarily about 'action', although theoretical perspectives can provide a helpful framework for the research design in terms of the structure of the research process. One of the founders of the approach, Kurt Lewin (1952), conceived the action research process as consisting of a 'spiral of cycles' which start with a general idea, followed by fact finding (reconnaissance) and the subsequent planning of action. After developing and implementing the first action step, evaluation takes place which informs the revision of the original plan. This model was refined further by Kemmis (1980), Elliott (1991), and Carr and Kemmis (1986), and can be translated into a more concrete timetable format, specifying the duration of the action and clearly stating the start and finish and the type of activities employed for data collection and evaluation. As illustrated in Figure 10.2 below, the insights gained from one cycle will subsequently be used to formulate the new need for change and plan the action of the next cycle.

The various models presented in the literature suggest that action research is a neat process made up of logically sequenced stages of activities. However, it can prove a 'messy business' (Cook, 1998), one which manifests itself in U-turns, cul-de-sacs, and off-shoots of new, emerging issues, which may also be worth pursuing but would detract from the original focus of the enquiry. Figure 10.3 provides a possible mapping and sequencing of discrete activities as they may occur in an action research cycle. Note that moving from an abstract model to its practical application in the 'real world' is not always straightforward.

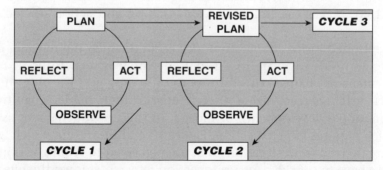

Figure 10.2 Action research model (adapted from Carr and Kemmis, 1986, *Becoming Critical: Knowing through Action Research*. Lewes: Falmer Press)

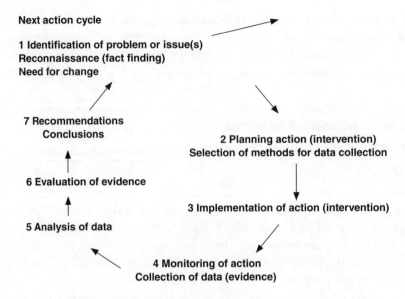

Figure 10.3   Activities inherent in an action cycle

Identifying a focus and planning a project

A number of parallel processes have to be undertaken when planning an action research project, all of which must be conducted in a systematic and coherent way and constructed around the focus that has been chosen for the enquiry. Much of this approach will be familiar to educators who have a natural empathy and a background training which helps them to reflect on the success of their teaching and learning. This can be both a help and a hindrance since it means that the general approach of identifying a potential area for improvement, taking action to make things better, and reflecting on outcomes is a familiar and natural element of professional practice. The problems come in making this approach systematic rather than intuitive. Table 10.1, which was originally constructed by Burton et al. (2008: 135), makes the links between teaching and action research more explicit.

As mentioned earlier, the general idea around which the research is to be constructed needs to relate to a situation which is seen to be in need of improvement or change. This mirrors the teaching and learning situation, in which teachers recognize a discrete area in their pupils' cognitive and socio-emotional development, or indeed, in their own behaviour as teachers, which requires targeted action. Figure 10.4 illustrates how such 'general ideas' are derived from situations that are perceived to require action.

When we have to consider an area for action research, it is worthwhile to take heed of Elliott's (1991: 72) caveat. First, the general idea needs to be related to our field of action as researchers and the situation to be improved must be

Table 10.1 Links between teaching and action research

Teaching	Action research
Topic of teaching unit or scheme of work	Focus of action enquiry (the issue, the problem)
Number of specific lessons	Number of action cycles
Resources required to teach the unit	Resources required to gather evidence
Identification of teacher and learner activities	Identification of researcher and participant activities
Nature of relationship between teacher and learner and how this affects the learning process	Positionality of the research and how this affects the behaviour of other research participants
Ethical considerations • Confidentiality of information • Balancing the need for information and pupil's right to privacy	Ethical considerations • Balance of power and control • Anonymity of participants • Confidentiality of information • Gaining informed consent
Selection of appropriate teaching/learning/assessment approach and strategies	Selection of appropriate research approach and strategies (quantitative/qualitative/mixed methodology)
Validity and reliability of assessment Multi-method approach in the generation of evidence for assessment	Validity and trustworthiness of research findings 'Multi-technique' (Elliott, 1991:77), triangulation by method, data, perspective, site
Awareness of structural, social, cultural factors inherent in the teaching/learning environment and their impact on the teaching/learning process	Identification of potential methodological, epistemological, ethical issues and their impact on the quality of the research
Monitoring of learner behaviour, attitude and critical incidents Gathering of evidence of learning: • Formal and informal • Formative and summative	Data collection (quantitative and qualitative), including use of 'analytic memos' (Elliott, 1991) to assist in the interpretation of data and to inform the next cycle
Evidence of learning outcomes (marks and narrative report)	Research evidence (quantitative and qualitative data)
Analysis and interpretation of assessment data	Analysis and interpretation of research data
Conclusions drawn with regard to informing teaching and learning strategies	Conclusions drawn with regard to informing professional practice

in need of such action based on the result of the action research. As researchers we must be prepared for unexpected findings to emerge which may change the original conception of the issues and redirect the research.

Example A:
Concerns have been identified about the extent to which the curriculum is fit for purpose and whether it engages students fully in order to lead to best outcomes. How can staff and students collaboratively explore heuristic and relevant approaches to teaching and learning?

Example B:
A primary school class teacher notes that the pupils in her class fail to collaborate well during school activities. How can they begin to develop key skills in collaboration with pupils, parents, teachers and other staff in the school?

Example C:
A headteacher is concerned about relationships and attitudes in the school both between staff and students and between students and students. How can she begin to develop and put into practice a policy that will begin to encourage more positive working relationships?

Figure 10.4   Starting points

However, in order to gain the best initial understanding of the situation Lewin's (1946) notion of 'reconnaissance' must precede any action research by finding out more about the particular situation that has been identified for improvement. If we return to the three examples given earlier, the reconnaissance phase may include asking the questions shown in Figure 10.5.

Example A:
What are the current aims of the curriculum?
How is the curriculum currently planned and organized?
What resources are being used to deliver the curriculum?
Are there any alternative curriculum materials available within the school or in network schools?
What is the budget for acquiring further resources?
What areas of the curriculum and approaches to teaching and learning do the pupils seem to like and dislike?
What approaches to teaching and learning seem most successful in terms of outcomes?
What further training is available for staff in this area?

Example B:
What are the specific problems in terms of collaboration?
At what point and why does collaboration seem to break down?
What current activities seem to work well and which activities are most problematic?
What positive examples of collaboration can be built upon?
What resources are available for new activities that encourage collaboration?
What expertise is available in the school or the wider network of schools?
What training is available?

Example C:
What specific problems can be identified in terms of behaviour and relationships?
What areas of the school cause particular concern?
What is the current behaviour/relationships policy for the school, when was it last reviewed, and who was involved in its formulation?
Which staff have specific responsibility for behaviour management?
Does the performance management policy of the school encourage positive relationships?
To what extent are parents and pupils involved in setting aims and goals for the school?

Figure 10.5   Formulating the research question

These questions can in turn inform the construction of the research questions and provide a basic structure around which to plan and conduct the actions. They can also give an indication of possible categories for the collection and analysis of data. By developing a catalogue of questions, our initial assumptions may be dispersed in light of the findings, resulting in a new interpretation of the situation to be investigated. Subsequently, our revised perception may perhaps give rise to a hypothesis, which according to Elliott will describe 'the situation', indicate a need for improvement or change, and explain the relationship between the two (see Figure 10.6).

Example A:
A more heuristic approach to teaching and learning can enhance pupils' learning experience and result in improved learning outcomes.

Example B:
The active involvement of pupils in planning learning activities can enhance collaboration.

Example C:
Positive behaviour can be encouraged through the development of a clear management policy that engages all stakeholders in the school.

Figure 10.6   Stating the hypothesis

Such hypotheses are not to be understood in the strictly scientific/positivistic sense which is either proved or disproved in the form of measurable quantitative data, since in the action research approach hypotheses are a device in which we can frame a critical enquiry into professional practice with the aim of gaining new insights into processes and acquiring a more profound understanding of the various complex factors influencing the teaching and learning process. Once the hypothesis has been formulated strategies for change need to be identified which can then be tried out, and a number of key questions will also have to be formulated and answered relating to the research process, such as:

- How many action cycles are needed?
- What should be included in each cycle, and what would be the duration of each of these?
- What would be the most appropriate start and finish date for each cycle keeping in mind the other pressures that are present in the institution, such as term dates, examination timetables, etc.?

It is at this point various professional considerations will need to be taken into consideration. Above all, we will need to bear in mind that the aim is to improve practice and not merely to undertake research. Since any action research will inevitably have some impact on the human 'subjects' that make up the life of an educational institution, whether they be staff or students, there is a paramount ethical requirement that as researchers we must ensure we are always confident that any action is in the best interests of the individuals involved. It is also equally important that all appropriate ethical procedures are followed, and that colleagues and subjects are made aware of what is being undertaken in the name of research. Basic common sense and normal professional standards will usually ensure that nothing untoward happens and that there are no problematic consequences, but the main points we must keep in mind are to:

- consult and inform colleagues/stakeholders about the research;
- gain permission and agreement from line managers and from staff and students wherever required;
- never undertake any actions that may be detrimental to the progress of students or the organization as a whole;
- always apply normal professional standards of behaviour and never to consider that the conduct of research gives us license to step outside such standards;
- maintain positive relationships with all the participants at all times;
- ensure the transparency of the research process by effectively communicating with all the parties involved;
- keep a detailed log of the research process;
- never apportion blame when things go wrong;
- be prepared to consider the views of others;
- appreciate the fact that teachers/lecturers are busy professionals and cannot always give of their time;
- be flexible and be prepared for the unexpected.

If we keep these basic principles in mind we should be able to avoid almost all problematic issues, but we must also remember that research of any kind may give rise to unforeseen consequences that we will then need to deal with. Many educational institutions will also have their own policies for the conduct of research, and action research may well be dealt with under strategies for educational improvement and integrated into institutional development plans.

Reporting action research

As we mentioned earlier one of the key requirements of action research is that its finding should be made public (Stenhouse, 1975). Such reporting may be at different levels and might include colleagues of the researcher at an institutional level in the hope that this will have an impact on practice across a department or sub-unit of the institution. More commonly, however, for the educational leader the aim will be to influence overall institutional practice and reporting will involve members of the senior management team, governors, fellow practitioners and other stakeholders. Professional researchers will inevitably have to report to a funding agency and thus may wish to disseminate their work more widely via its publication in professional or academic journals. Regardless of the 'level' of reporting, the aim will be to impact on professional practice in the classroom, across departments or across several schools, in the way in which professional practice is reviewed, analyzed and reassessed (Burton et al., 2008).

Summary ☐

The processes involved in action research are not dissimilar to those inherent in teaching and in educational improvement, and should therefore come naturally to any institutional leader who is committed to the development of their workplace. However, action research does not always progress in the linear fashion that is so neatly shown in the various figures above, which tend to illustrate a simplistic notion of problem identification, action, review and improvement. In fact action research is particularly prone to setting off in unexpected directions since the action itself may produce unexpected and sometimes unwelcome results (Dickens and Watkins, 1999). For this reason any researcher who considers engaging in this approach needs to be realistic in terms of the scope of the project and about what can be achieved in a given amount of time and resources in a particular practice setting. The actions of any institutional leader can sometimes be interpreted as being threatening by those that they manage, and problematic by those to whom they are answerable, and action research may itself induce such reactions. In such situations action research can be perceived differently by the various stakeholders and may even be misconstrued as subversive. It is therefore important that as researchers we consult widely and produce regular update reports on our progress in order to ensure that such problems are kept to a minimum. Nonetheless, action research remains one of the most popular approaches to educational research because of the potential it holds in terms of improving practice.

Further reading

Greenwood, D.J. and Levin, M. (2006) *Introduction to Action Research.* Thousand Oaks, CA: Sage.

Koshy, V. (2009) *Action Research For Improving Educational Practice: A Step-By-Step Guide.* London: Sage.

McNiff, J. and Whitehead, J. (2009) *Doing and Writing Action Research.* London: Sage.

McNiff, J. and Whitehead, J. (2011) *All You Need To Know About Action Research.* London: Sage.

Stringer, E. (2007) *Action Research.* Thousand Oaks, CA: Sage.

Part 3

Analyzing data and reporting the findings of research in educational institutions

11

Analyzing Quantitative Data

Aims

Analysis is needed to convert data into findings, and different research projects with different data collection methods will yield data needing different treatments in analysis. Analysis is clearly a key element in any research project and it needs to be planned and considered in detail in the design phase of the research. In questionnaire research it is essential that as a researcher you decide well in advance of the data collection how you will analyze your data rather than collecting these and then hoping that a means to analyze can suddenly and fortuitously be located at a later date. The notion of analyzing quantitative data tends to conjure up visions of complex and unending statistical tests. However, if you find the prospect of statistics daunting we would advise you not to be too alarmed, as much analysis of quantitative data can be undertaken simply and result in familiar tables, graphs, pie-charts, percentages and the like. Straightforward analysis of this type can yield high quality findings which are credible and can make a full contribution to advancing the knowledge base in the field of leadership studies, and in this chapter we aim to set out the use of descriptive statistics of this kind. There will also be designs and occasions when as a researcher you will need to undertake more complex analysis using inferential statistical tests (for example, if a statistical difference needs to be established between the means of two sets of data), so in addition we will provide you with a workable introduction to some commonly used statistical tests in order that making decisions about their suitability for use in analysis can be an easier task. (A carefully chosen further reading list offers you continued guidance if this inferential statistics route is appropriate for a particular research project where you are seeking to establish statistically significant differences between groups and data sets.) Finally, the chapter aims to alert you to the increasing use of experiments as a research method in some countries, the kind of data that may emerge, and how that data may be analyzed. By the end of this chapter you should be able to:

- understand when and why questionnaires are the best way to undertake research;
- have a strong grasp of the issues associated with descriptive and inferential statistics.

Using questionnaires

When you are using questionnaires in research, although textual sections may be included, data are most likely to be collected in the form of numbers (see Chapter 6). Other methods available to you, such as controlled trials, are also likely to present you with numerical data. In this chapter we turn our attention to the reality that numerical data will need to be analyzed as part of research; and that such analysis is necessary to establish findings and present them to whoever will access the completed research report. In their *Hard Pressed Researcher* textbook, Edwards and Talbot remind us that:

> Whether you are undertaking survey research, using open-ended questions on a questionnaire, gathering interview data, using descriptive observation methods or simply gathering a variety of forms of written material as data, the time will come when you will have to cease these squirrel-like activities and begin to make sense of the material that is accumulating around you. (1994: 102)

So what constitutes analysis and what will you need need to do here? Denscombe suggests that analysis can be defined as follows:

> Analysis means the separation of something into its component parts. To do this, of course, the researcher first needs to identify what those parts might be, and this links with a further meaning of analysis, which is to trace things back to their underlying sources. Analysis, then, involves probing beneath the surface appearance of something to discover the component elements which have come together to produce it. By tracing things back in this fashion, the researcher hopes to expose some *general* principles that can be used to explain the nature of the thing being studied and can be applied elsewhere to other situations. (2003: 299)

In focusing on the analysis of quantitative data we would put forward the use of descriptive statistics as a straightforward way to analyze and present numerical data. Descriptive statistics, such as percentages, means and standard deviations, graphs and pie-charts, frequently appear in educational research papers, theses and dissertations, and can be used to excellent effect to analyze and present findings in many studies. In other studies, the use of inferential statistics or 'statistical tests' to analyze and present 'statistically significant' findings will be appropriate, but only if they have a role to play in the purpose of the research and its intentions. The application of statistical tests need not be worrying, and it is intended that this chapter will demonstrate how and when they may be used. It is likely that the use of descriptive and inferential statistics will be associated with data emerging from the closed questions within questionnaires. If, however, textual data is obtained via the use of open questionnaire questions (see Chapter 6) then the advice offered within this book pertaining to the analysis of quantitative data will be more appropriate.

Numerical data and descriptive statistics

Denscombe (2003) reminds us that research data may well come in the form of numbers and be suitable for relatively simple analysis (for example, a percentage who agree and a percentage who do not agree). Let us assume that you have administered a questionnaire with 20 closed questions/statements, each answered on a 1 (strongly disagree) to 5 (strongly agree) scale, and a number of possibilities for analysis then emerge. A straightforward analysis could include:

- collating the responses from each of the 20 statements into the five categories ranging from 1 to 5 and presenting these as a table of percentages;
- presenting the percentages for each statement as a bar chart or pie chart;
- calculating the mean (the average) and the mode (the most popular) for each statement;
- choosing the four (or five) highest means and modes to discuss;
- choosing the four (or five) lowest means and modes to discuss;
- calculating the standard deviation (to give an indication of the spread of the responses to each statement) for each statement;
- choosing the four (or five) statements with the highest standard deviations to discuss;
- choosing the four (or five) statements with the lowest standard deviations to discuss.

These items all represent *descriptive statistics* and enable an analysis that can assist a discussion of the 'socially significant' findings. They show analyses that are easy to perform and will yield helpful findings and subsequent discussion. (We will elaborate here on the term 'standard deviation' in case you are unfamiliar with this.)

Calculating standard deviation gives a measure of the spread of the data from the mean. Sometimes data will show that all the values obtained are close to the mean, sometimes there will be a great difference in score values with huge variation between individual scores and some may not reside close to the mean. This variation is known as the standard deviation. This can be seen in Figure 11.1.

The manner in which data analyzed using descriptive statistics are presented is something that many researchers will be familiar with. Its aim is to make the analyzed data appear clear and accessible. As such it can include:

- tables;
- rank orders of items;
- vertical or horizontal bar charts to present frequencies;
- histograms to present frequencies;

This variation is known as the standard deviation. This can be illustrated using the table shown below:

Imagine a list of scores to be 1, 6, 8, 10, 17 and 18. The mean (average) is found by adding them up and dividing by the number of scores i.e. 60 divided by 6 = 10.

Score	Score – Mean	Difference from Mean	Squared Difference
1	1 – 10	–9	81
6	6 – 10	–4	16
8	8 – 10	–2	4
10	10 – 10	0	0
17	17 – 10	+7	49
18	18 – 10	+8	64
		Total 0	Total 214

By squaring the difference from the mean there is a measure of the variation of the scores. The sum of squares, in this case 214, is divided by the number of degrees of freedom (the total number of scores minus one), and then the square root is taken, giving in this case a value of 6.54.

Sum of squares   214
Number of scores   6
Degrees of freedom   5   214/5 = 42.8
The square root of 42.8   6.54 (to three significant figures)

So the standard deviation (SD) is 6.54, making the mean and standard deviation to be 10 plus or minus 6.54.

The general formula used for calculating standard deviation is:

$$SD = \sqrt{\frac{\text{sum of squares of individual differences from the mean}}{\text{degrees of freedom}}}$$

Figure 11.1   Standard deviation

- scatter plots to show the extent of a relationship (correlation) between two variables;
- line graphs to show trends in the data;
- pie-charts to show the relative size of the categories generated.

We need to elaborate here on the term 'correlation'. A correlation, or mutual connection, can be shown in the form of a scatter plot (see below) detailing the relationship between two or more variables. This technique can then be extended to provide a statistical estimate of the strength of correlation between the two variables. The statistical expression of the association between the two variables is known as the 'coefficient of correlation'. Two variables are said to be correlated when an increase in one variable is accompanied by an increase in the other (a positive correlation) or decrease (a negative correlation) in the other. Below we show two simple example scatter plots which demonstrate the likely close correlation between variables A and B.

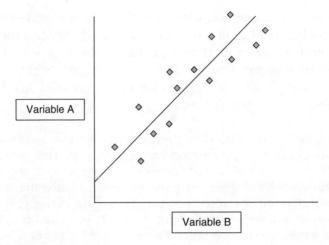

Figure 11.2   A positive correlation

In Figure 11.2 the correlation is positive because both variables are increasing together.

In Figure 11.3 the correlation is negative because an increase in one variable is accompanied by a decrease in the other.

A straightforward summation of data and the calculation of values such as means can easily be undertaken using spreadsheets that are available on computers. Spreadsheets will allow you to enter numerical data using actual numbers or numerical codes that have been ascribed to items of data (see Jarvis, 2011). Spreadsheets can also help you organize data, and with software additions they can produce items such as tables and bar charts as well.

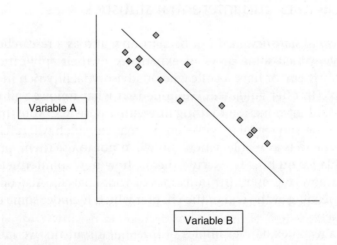

Figure 11.3   A negative correlation

Coding the data from questionnaires in this way was undertaken by Dr Adrian Jarvis, a former PhD student of one of the authors, who studied the interaction between subject leaders and their staff in a variety of secondary school departments. He engaged a mixed-methods approach, including interviews, questionnaires and observation. The following extract from his thesis (Jarvis, 2011: 140) gives some details of this:

> In analysing the questionnaire data, the first stage, as Munn and Drever (1995) counsel, was to put them into a more manageable form. This meant creating a series of computer spreadsheets containing 'grids' into which the answers to closed, numerically-based questions could be placed. Coding the answers was thus a straightforward operation, since, as Munn and Drever (1995) remind us, "the categories of response [were] preset" (p. 42). For scaled questions, each respondent was assigned a number and answers coded either by a letter ("Y" = "yes") or a number ("1" = most preferred choice) as appropriate. Open questions were coded according to a system of what Munn and Drever (1995) call, "categories derived from the data" (p. 45). As these two authors say, this calls for the researcher to, "take a batch of responses", and then "summarise each into a few simple statements", before trying to "group similar statements together, decide what they have in common, and so define the categories into which... the answers might naturally fall (p. 45).

In summary, utilizing descriptive statistics will enable you to undertake an analysis that can relate to a discussion of the 'socially significant' findings. However, if you want to identify those findings which are 'statistically significant' as well as 'socially significant', then you will need to use inferential statistics. In short, differential statistics can help you describe and inferential statistics can help you deduce.

Numerical data and inferential statistics

Using *inferential statistics* need not be alarming, and as a researcher you may already have gained some previous experience of their application, learned how to apply them, or have a colleague or advisory facility rich in experience and available to offer guidance. We hope that what follows will offer you a straightforward introduction to using inferential statistics. Note that there are many accessible and readable books on the market which will offer you information on the tests available, when and when not to use them, provide step-by-step guidance on how to execute them, show how to interpret outcomes, and suggest how to present the outcomes of your analysis. Also take a look at the further reading at the end of the chapter which includes some of the most useful of these.

In beginning to explore examples of inferential statistics we must first say something about the mathematical terms applied to data, as these will sometimes be used in relation to particular tests. In short, the data you collect may be nominal, ordinal, interval, or ratio. 'Nominal data' indicates that there is a difference between categories: for example, questionnaire data may yield answers that are either 'yes' or 'no'. 'Ordinal data' indicates that the size of a number has a meaning: for example, a score of 5 would indicate that a middle leader is a more skilled administrator than a middle leader who scored 1. 'Interval data' indicates that the distances between the numbers on a scale are the same: for example, data pertaining to the year 2000, 2001, 2002, and so on. 'Ratio data' are slightly different from 'interval data', because in the case of ratio data there is a true zero or reference point (see Pell and Fogelman, 2007).

Inferential statistics may be divided into *parametric statistics* and *non-parametric statistics*. Parametric statistics are undertaken with ratio and fixed interval data drawn from a normal population. Non-parametric tests are undertaken with nominal data (counting items and putting them into a category) and ordinal data (where categories are used but the intervals are not equal, for example Likert scales in a questionnaire), both of which show no particular pattern or distribution. It is frequently stated in the research literature (see, for example, Munn and Drever, 1995; Denscome, 2003) that minimum samples of 30 are required for the use of inferential statistics. Whilst this is a good 'rule of thumb', the research literature pertaining to the use of statistical tests also indicates that non-parametric tests can be used on smaller data sets in some circumstances. There is limited value in communicating the fine details on the execution of each individual test within this chapter, as a wide variety of books and an array of available software (for example, the Statistical Package for the Social Sciences – SPSS) will do the calculations for you; however, we do believe that an introductory review of commonly used tests will help you decide if a particular test may or may not be relevant to your needs. This illustrated introductory review is presented below.

Examples of parametric statistical tests

There are two examples of parametric tests that may be of help in your leadership research:

1. The t-test.
2. Analysis of Variance (ANOVA).

The t-test

As a researcher you may want to compare two sets of data to establish if there is a statistically significant difference between them. For example, in seeking to compare the scores obtained from a group who have received a treatment (e.g. training) and a control group who have not received the treatment (e.g. no training) then a t-test can be applied. The t-test requires the calculation of the means and standard deviations of the two data sets (see above). It then compares the means and any overlap in the variation within the two data sets, and offers a figure which can be compared to tables of probability (p) values to establish the level of statistical significance in the difference between the two means. The smaller the p value obtained, the more likely that the difference is statistically significant, and therefore that any difference is not easily attributed to a chance occurrence when comparing the data sets. For example, a (p) value of less than or equal to 0.001 means that this outcome would only have occurred a single time out of one thousand by chance, and therefore as a researcher you can have confidence that a real difference does exist between the two means.

Analysis of Variance (ANOVA)

Whilst the t-test is useful, it is limited in its use to two data groups as described above (i.e. only two levels of the independent variable). In cases where there are multiple levels of the independent variable, performing multiple t-tests to look for differences between means should not be used: rather, a procedure called analysis of variance (ANOVA) must be called upon. Analysis of variance (ANOVA) can be conducted using the Statistical Package for the Social the Social Sciences (SPSS) and will yield accessible data pertaining to the statistical significance, or otherwise, of the differences between the means of data sets (Field, 2009; Pallant, 2010).

Examples of non-parametric statistical tests

Here are three examples of non-parametric tests that may be helpful in leadership research:

1. The Chi-square test.
2. The Median Sign test.
3. The Kruskal-Wallis test.

The Chi-square test

Statistical tests provide a measure for the probability of a relationship between data sets reflecting the variables under consideration. Researchers and statisticians will sometimes use the term the 'null hypothesis' to indicate that there is no relationship between the variables. This is the stance held until an appropriate test is applied to the data and the analysis indicates that a significant difference really does exist. One of the most commonly used tests to find out if two variables are associated to a significant level or not is the Chi-square test. The

Chi-square test is based upon the difference between what is observed and what is expected. For example, if left entirely to chance (i.e. there were no influence factors at play that might skew the response), then mathematically you would expect a 50:50 distribution of response, for example, between those who agree with a particular premise and those who do not agree with it. Imagine that individuals are responding to the same statements presented as a Likert scale within a questionnaire. The responses to the statements may indicate that they 'agree' or that they 'disagree' with a statement made. Each question will generate the numbers 'agreeing' or 'disagreeing'. On examining these numbers the researcher may find that the distribution of response is not close to 50:50 and therefore some influence may be at work in determining the response pattern obtained. Is the distribution obtained different from that which may be obtained by chance? Can any difference be shown to be a statistically significantly difference? The Chi-square test will calculate this.

Examples from our own work show Chi-square being used within the context of leadership research. For example, Rhodes, Hollinshead and Nevill (2007) used a Chi-square test to investigate aspects of the job satisfaction of academic staff working in two different universities. The research utilized questionnaires to establish which facets of their work they deemed most influential in determining their job satisfaction. A rank order of these facets from highest to lowest was then created. A Chi-square test was then used to establish if these responses were either significantly deeply satisfying or significantly deeply dissatisfying to the respondents. All numerical data were entered onto a spreadsheet and the level of significance was set at $p \leq 0.005$. A small illustrative extract from the full findings is shown in Table 11.1.

In all the examples displayed, the Chi-square test revealed a probability value (p) showing that the observed distribution between the two categories of deeply satisfying and deeply dissatisfying was statistically significant.

Table 11.1 Rank Order of Facets Deemed Deeply Satisfying or Deeply Dissatisfying

Facet	Respondents	Deeply Satisfying	Deeply Dissatisfying	P	Significance
Friendliness of colleagues	34	33	1	0.0000	Significant
Collaborative working	33	29	4	0.0000	Significant
Proportion of time spent on administration	27	0	27	0.0000	Significant
Opportunities for self-management	26	24	2	0.0000	Significant
Intellectual challenge	25	25	0	0.0000	Significant

The Median Sign test

The Median Sign test can be used to test whether the responses given in each category of a Likert scale are random or whether there is a significant pattern. In the case shown below it provides a comparison between those responding more positively than expected with those responding more negatively than expected. In the same research project concerned with the job satisfaction of university academics in two different universities, Rhodes et al. (2007) identified 35 facets that were likely to impact upon job satisfaction. The importance of each facet to the academics was expressed by them using a five-point Likert scale that allowed them to specify whether individual facets were of *high importance, importance, neutral, low importance* or *no importance* in relation to their job satisfaction. By setting the neutral null hypothesis as three within the five-point Likert scale, a median sign test could be used to establish for which of the facets the neutral null hypothesis should be either accepted or rejected. Again, the level of significance was set at $p=0.005$. A small illustrative extract from the full findings is shown in Table 11.2. (Note that the table collapses *high importance* and *importance* into a single category and *low importance* or *no importance* into a single category.)

Table 11.2 Rank Order of Facets Deemed Important or Not Important

Facet	Respondents	Important	Neutral	Not Important	P	Significance
Students are well-motivated	68	64	3	1	0.0000	Significant
The salary is appropriate	68	58	7	3	0.0000	Significant
Recognition of my efforts	68	61	5	2	0.0000	Significant
Proportion of time spent on administration	67	46	16	5	0.0000	Significant
Physical condition of the working environment	68	55	11	2	0.0000	Significant
Prestige derived from association with your university	68	22	31	5	0.3240	Not Significant
Society's views of lecturers	68	14	38	16	0.8555	Not Significant

This shows five facets reflecting a significant deviation from the null hypothesis and two facets not showing a significant difference. In short, the first five facets are perceived to be influential in impacting on job satisfaction, whereas the latter two facets are deemed less important.

The Kruskal-Wallis test

Non-parametric statistics should be used when dealing with ordinal data. A non-parametric Kruskal-Wallis test may be used to show any significant difference between data emanating from different respondent groups who provide data by completing Likert scales in questionnaires. Rhodes et al. (2008) found that a combined sample of 429 headteachers, middle leaders and classroom teachers, drawn from sample schools in England, identified 20 characteristics thought to be important in indicating leadership talent. A Kruskal-Wallis Test was used to explore any variation in the perception of heads, middle leaders and classroom teachers within the sample with respect to the degree of importance these individual groups attached to the identified characteristics. The level of significance was set at $p \leq 0.005$. A small illustrative extract from the full findings is shown in Table 11.3.

Table 11.3 Rank Order of Facets Deemed Significant or Not Significant

Characteristic of Leadership Talent	P	Significance	Finding
Shows initiative	0.411	Not Significant	No Significant Difference in Perception
Has vision	0.027	Not Significant	No Significant Difference in Perception
Shows confidence	0.088	Not Significant	No Significant Difference in Perception
Has people skills	0.077	Not Significant	No Significant Difference in Perception
Is a competent teacher	0.001	Significant	More Important to Middle Leaders than Heads or Classroom Teachers
Has good communication skills	0.138	Not Significant	No Significant Differences in Perception
Shows ambition	0.002	Significant	More Important to Classroom Teachers and Middle Leaders than to Heads
Shows enthusiasm	0.002	Significant	More Important to Heads than to Middle Leaders or Classroom Teachers

This shows that there was no significant difference in response from the three groups with respect to five of the characteristics, but significant difference was found with respect to three of the characteristics. This finding enabled a discussion of why the difference in response between groups may have occurred.

Randomized controlled trials in the analysis of experimental data

In seeking to establish, in an unbiased way, whether educational interventions are effective in improving learner outcomes, you may wish to consider the use of an experimental group (exposed to the intervention) and a control group (not exposed to the intervention) in your research design. Control groups could be established by seeking to match individual learners or groups of learners. For example, two high performing year 6 groups in primary school showing clear similarities in terms of composition and setting may be selected. One of these groups could act as an experimental group and one as a control group. Individuals within the groups may then be randomly selected to help minimise any selection bias (see Chapter 5). Torgerson (2009) points out that this kind of educational research has gained much more international attention in the past few years as a basis upon which to inform decision making at all levels within the education system. An international interest in a more 'scientific' approach is apparent in the research literature. Randomized controlled trials are described as an evaluative method used by social scientists in order to establish whether an intervention such as a programme or practice is effective or not. Torgerson describes a recently undertaken randomized controlled trial to investigate whether an ICT intervention was effective in improving the literacy of 11 and 12 year-old children. She concludes that well-designed trials are crucial to the development of evidence-based education.

So how might such experimental data be analyzed? An example of possible analysis is offered by an investigation of 'effect size' (see Joyce, Calhoun and Hopkins, 1999; Coe, 2002). Imagine that a group of students is split randomly into two sub-groups with the first group following a conventional route through their programme (i.e. the 'control' group) and the second group (i.e. the 'experimental' group) being subjected to a new intervention. Hopefully a baseline test would show no difference between the two sub-groups at the start of the experiment, but has the treatment influenced the outcome of measured performance such as an examination or test at the end of their programme? 'Effect size' is a simple way of quantifying the difference between two such groups (see Figure 11.4).

$$\text{Effect Size} = \frac{\text{Average (experimental group)} - \text{Average (control group)}}{\text{Standard Deviation of the Control Group}}$$

Figure 11.4 Calculating Effect Size

Coe (2002) offers an interpretive table and advice on how to assess the effect size calculated and what significance this might have for concluding the success of the intervention or otherwise. Data showing large effect sizes will be most effective in establishing the findings' importance.

Summary

This chapter offered insights into the analysis and presentation of numerical data. Although of an introductory nature, we hope that sufficient guidance was provided to enable you to access and understand ideas and techniques appropriate to the analysis of quantitative data, and enable you to make judgements concerning the use of such analysis within your intended research projects. A great deal of information is available to researchers on how to execute statistical tests, how to interpret outcomes, and how to present the outcomes of the analysis. (See some of the most useful texts in the suggested further reading list at the end of this chapter.) The chapter also explored and illustrated the use of means and standard deviations and how variables may be correlated. Parametric tests such as the t-test and ANOVA were included as were non-parametric tests such as the Chi-square test, the Median Sign test, and the Kruskal-Wallis test. The analysis of experimental data was also considered. Finally, we emphasized that increasingly user-friendly calculators and computer software were now available in abundance and it was reassuring researchers to know that much of the mathematical manipulation formerly required in analyzing quantitative data could now be achieved with the use of some well-chosen key strokes.

Further reading

Connolly, P. (2007) *Quantitative Data Analysis in Education: A Critical Introduction Using SPSS.* London: Routledge.

Field, A. (2009) *Discovering Statistics Using SPSS* (3rd edition). London: Sage.

Gorard, S. (2001) *Quantitative Methods in Educational Research: The Role of Numbers Made Easy.* London: Continuum.

Hinton, P., Brownlow, C. and McMurray, I. (2004) *SPSS Explained* (2nd edition). London: Routledge.

Pallant, J. (2010) *SPSS Survival Manual: A Step by Step Guide to Data Analysis using SPSS.* Maidenhead: Open University Press.

12

Analyzing Qualitative Data

Aims

In the last chapter we considered different ways of selecting and presenting quantitative data with the aim of providing a clear overview and in preparation for analyzing the information gathered. By the end of this chapter you should have developed an understanding of the principles underpinning qualitative data analysis and how it forms a bridge between data collection, interpretation and development of theory. Specifically, you should:

- understand the overall process of analyzing qualitative data;
- grasp the main approaches to qualitative data analysis;
- understand and be able to follow the main steps in qualitative data analysis;
- be aware of the challenges that qualitative data may pose for the researcher;
- realize the importance of validity, reliability and trustworthiness in qualitative as well as quantitative research.

The process of analyzing qualitative data

No one brief chapter can address the many ways in which qualitative data can be analyzed, but the overall process has been shown to consist of three main elements which Miles and Huberman (1994: 10) describe as 'three concurrent flows of activity'. These include:

> *Data reduction* – which refers to the process of selecting, focusing, simplifying, and abstracting the data that appear in field notes, or transcriptions of data that may be derived from interviews, observations or other qualitative research tools (ibid: 10).
>
> *Data display* – which is an organized, compressed assembly of information that allows the researcher to make inferences and draw conclusions (ibid: 11).

Conclusion drawing and verification – is the process whereby the researcher notes regularities, discerns patterns, makes explanations, notes causal flows, and outlines propositions derived from the data (ibid: 11).

The fact that these three elements operate concurrently means, of course, that they occur at the same time, and as a researcher you should note that there is a subtle interplay between the different but overlapping and interconnected processes. This is because all three activities take place throughout a piece of qualitative research and not solely, as some novice researchers may presume, at the end of a research project. This is one of many differences between the process of analyzing qualitative and quantitative data since, in the latter approach, although the same three processes take place, it is a rule that they will be performed sequentially and not concurrently. In part, this is due to the differing philosophical stances adopted by qualitative and quantitative researchers that were discussed in Chapters 1 and 2, but it is also relates to the differing practices in the collection of data that are inherent in these two approaches to research. The research tools employed by quantitative researchers, such as questionnaires, or the noting of frequencies in observation which can be reduced to numeric scores, mean that the data tend to remain an abstract series of numbers which must be processed in a systematic and sequential manner. For the qualitative researcher, the very nature of the data, which may be in the form of notes or recordings of conversations and discussions, means that the researcher cannot avoid beginning to reflect on what they have seen and heard from the moment those data begin to be gathered. This means that the qualitative researcher will 'shuttle' between the four nodes of data collection, data reduction, data display, and conclusion drawing throughout a research study (Miles and Huberman, 1994: 12). Nonetheless, you need to remember that there *is* a sequence to qualitative analysis and, although as a researcher you will begin to undertake the process of drawing conclusions during data gathering and as the evidence begins to emerge, you will only be able to draw your final conclusions once you have gathered all of the data.

Approaches to qualitative data analysis

As a researcher you may choose from a variety of different approaches to qualitative data analysis, all of which have things in common but are different in their philosophical approach. A number of these approaches were outlined earlier in the book, but if we revisit just four of these we may see both similarities and differences:

- *Ethnography*, which is the study of the culture of a group or groups of people. This involves participant observation where the researcher immerses him- or her-self in the culture of the organization being studied. This approach is likely to produce data in the form of field notes and diaries.

- *Ethnomethodology*, which also involves the study of a culture and will require sustained involvement in the organization being studied. However, whereas the ethnologist will try to analyze and describe the world as the participants see it, the ethnomethodologist will try to maintain some distance from the subjects of the research. Note that ethnomethodologists do not necessarily believe that they can be completely objective or generate generalizable and universal findings, but their focus is on the way that the people within a cultural setting construct and create the world they live in. Data are also likely to be in the form of diaries, observations and field notes.
- *Grounded theory*, which involves developing theory inductively through observations of a given setting. The observations are eventually developed into categories which are continually re-examined against further observations, and then compared with and linked to other categories.
- *Narrative analysis*, which tries to analyze and construct the narrative or story that is being told by respondents. It is most commonly used with data derived from interviews.

We may note that data derived from qualitative research may come in many forms, such an interview transcripts, notes and recordings from focus groups, field notes, diaries, notes on observations, etc. The data may arise from a single source or many sources, and these sources might all be within one organization or distributed amongst a number of organizations, often in the form of a series of case studies. The thing that all of this material will have in common is that the data will be in the form of words (or *text* as it more commonly called).

Whether in regard to quantitative or qualitative data, coding is generally used as a means of identifying key material in the data in order to allocate it to a system of categories and sub-categories. We generally differentiate between pre-determined codes, which can be derived from the literature or existing models and frameworks, and open codes, which emerge naturally from the data during collection, analysis and interpretation. While the former is more akin to a deductive approach, the latter is used inductively. In this sense coding is not be understood exclusively as a technical activity but as an organic, interactive process, and one that also includes the use of literature as highlighted by Strauss and Corbin (1998: 49–52). They hold that concepts emerging from the data can be compared in terms of their properties and dimensions, and that our reading of the literature can act as a sensitising device, making the researcher aware of subtle nuances in the data. It can also be used to explore, confirm, and clarify the concepts used in categorizing material. Note, however, that in addition to this you will need to draw on your professional practice knowledge and personal experience to ensure that the codes and categories used in your analysis of the data are valid and meaningful (Eraut, 1994).

For example, by listening to interview recordings prior to, during and after coding, and reading transcripts and interview responses line by line, and word by word, you can analyze texts in a rigorous and systematic manner. Accordingly, 'data are broken down, conceptualized and put together in new ways', a process within which 'one's own and other's assumptions are explored and leading to new discoveries' (Strauss and Corbin, 1990: 57–62). Thus the categories for analysis can be derived from a variety of sources, including your own assumptions, hunches and hypotheses, as well as allowing for the emergence of new concepts (Tesch, 1990).

Despite the potential multiplicity of sources that qualitative researchers may be dealing with, there are a number of major steps in dealing with data that are common across sources. These key steps are outlined below.

Steps in analyzing qualitative data

Becoming familiar with the data

Becoming familiar with the material that you have gathered is the first and probably the most important stage in analysis. It involves a careful reading and re-reading of the text in order to gain initial insights and so begin to make connections. At this stage you can also engage in what is sometimes termed the *pre-coding* of the data. This may involve simple mental reflection and note making about parts of the text that might fit within pre-determined themes, and your identification of emergent themes that will begin to become apparent but which you did not necessarily envisage prior to gathering the data or identify in the literature. It may also involve you in making notes, underlining text, highlighting sections that may be of importance, etc.

Coding and categorizing

In qualitative research the terms 'coding' and 'categorizing' are often used co-terminously. In quantitative research this process involves assigning numerical codes in order to label variables with preset codes or values. This is not the case in the interpretivist approach since there you will not be seeking to make generalizable and universal claims. You may use numbers but these are usually a simple device to avoid the necessity of using further text or letters. However, it is noticeable that many researchers will use key words and mnemonic or other devices which will represent the labels ascribed to themes (such as *SI* for *School Improvement*, *INSET* for *In Service Training*, etc.).

In essence, you will be looking for patterns within the data which will suggest that an identifiable *theme* can be discerned which seems to be referred to as being of importance by one respondent or by several respondents or cases. At this stage you may well identify *pre-set themes or categories* which you would expect to be present because they were in the literature, but you might also note *emergent themes or categories* which you did not necessarily expect to be present but which emerge from the data in the process of analysis.

As a researcher you may also be able to identify *sub-themes* within major themes: these will require the development of further labels that might include the original label for the overall theme, plus the new label for the sub-theme (such as *SI/ RoH* for *School Improvement/Role of Headteacher*, *INSET/ LD* for *In-Service Training/Leadership Development*).

This process should continue until you have examined the data exhaustively for all themes and sub-themes.

Below is an example of simple coding based on an interview with a headteacher involved in a research project on curriculum innovation. The original research questions for the project included:

1. What key skills are required in leading curriculum innovation?
2. How can innovation be encouraged and developed in challenging circumstances?
3. What are the main characteristics of best practice in the leadership of curriculum innovation in primary schools?
4. To what extent is there a link between curriculum innovation and school effectiveness and improvement?
5. To what extent are schools ready to implement curriculum change?

The initial coding labels that were developed included codes based on themes derived from the research questions:

LI – Leadership issues
EI – Encouraging Innovation
LC – Leadership Characteristics
CISI – Curriculum Innovation and School Improvement
CR – Change Readiness

The codes based on emergent themes were:

TA – Thematic Approach
PR – Planning and Review
RR – Recording and Reporting
P – Piloting
BB – Breadth and Balance
RI – Resource Issues
SD – Strategy Development

The researcher may then feel that a number of categories and sub-categories can be identified as follows:

Formally, we've had one staff meeting to introduce planning and one	PR
to review it. But informally, we've had lots of incidental discussions.	
That's probably where all the thinking and tweaking and, you know,	EI
where all the real change is happening. Similarly we've looked at	RR
how we're recording children's work. You embark on this journey	
and you discover that it really does touch all areas of teaching and	
learning in the school. And, as we go through this year, there are	
things which are coming up all the time …. like so we haven't got	
13 subjects any more. We've got seven or eight areas of learning	
and that's obviously going to affect the subject leadership structure	CR
and then that's going to affect how we're assessing children. It's	
enormous …. because then so much has to change. And yet, not	
losing all the good practice that's been going on in the school for the	LI/ LC
last 10 or 12 years. It's a matter of holding on to all the good bits.	

*We started all this in January. So it's only last year and we had
two terms of grappling with where we wanted to go. So we've
implemented a themed approach to curriculum as a kind of pilot*   TA
*from September, based on what were the proposed progressions in
learning for each area of learning at that point. But for the purposes
of this research it cannot be underestimated just how much time
schools need for thinking before actually doing it and I need to make*   RI
*sure that time is found to do this. We had two terms of just thinking
about it and getting our heads round what this new curriculum might*   P
*look like. We then initiated a pilot for a year because you need to
run through an annual cycle of just trying things and tweaking and
adapting.*   CR

*By next September we're not going to be at a destination point but
I think we're going to be closer to actually having something that
we'll be running with.*   SD

*It's all about developing a strategy really. We have a two-year rolling
programme of themes that we have decided upon at this stage. In
future, we might want the children to come up with the themes. But*   BB
*as a starting point we've mapped out two years' worth of themes. We
wanted to ensure that we had a breadth across the different areas of*   CISI
*learning. So, some might be more scientifically focused whilst others
may be more historical. We also wanted to make sure that there were
opportunities for issues like globalisation and having a global view
of the world. We also wanted opportunities to be created for different*   CR
*cultural themes and extend the children's differing cultural experiences.
So, over two years we wanted to present a diet of themes which run
across each of the six areas of learning.*

Figure 12.1 Coding the transcript from an interview on the topic of curriculum innovation

Of course this is an interpretive, inexact and subjective process, since several sub-categories could be allocated under any one of the main categories. For instance, Resource Issues may well be relevant to all three main categories. Equally, Planning and Review may be subsumed under curriculum innovation. For this reason, a researcher needs to be prepared to continue to review

Table 12.1   Categories and sub-categories

Categories	Sub-categories
Leadership Issues	• Leadership characteristics • Resource issues • Strategy development
Curriculum Innovation	• Encouraging innovation • Curriculum innovation and school improvement • Thematic approach • Breadth and balance
Change	• Change readiness • Planning and review • Recording and reporting • Piloting

the categories and sub-categories as the work of analysis proceeds, and these may not become fixed until the end of the process when a full list of categories and sub-categories can be enumerated as in Table 12.1, above.

Identifying connections within and between categories and cases

Once the data have been coded and placed into themes or categories, you will have to look for patterns between and across such categories and, where relevant, across cases. For instance, the researcher who identified the importance of School Improvement and the In-Service Training may have also noted that these two themes were actually interconnected, since a number of respondents pointed out that school improvement strategies seemed to be enhanced by the availability of in-service training activities, and there may be further evidence that certain types of training were proving especially helpful in enhancing improvement. The use of matrices can be particularly helpful here, and these may range from a simple series of boxes that will allow the researcher to compare the data between categories, to complex matrices that will compare data that have been placed into different categories relating to different cases.

In the matrix below in Table 12.2 the researcher can place relevant data for each category under the different cases from which data have been gathered.

Table 12.2   Matrix comparing categories across cases

	Case 1	Case 2	Case 3	Case 4
Leadership Issues				
Curriculum Innovation				
Change				

This simple matrix can be elaborated by a further sub-division for sub-categories or for individuals within cases. In leadership research such matrices might take account of key factors such as:

- roles (principals, headteachers, deputy-headteachers, heads of department, class teachers/lecturers, newly qualified teachers/lecturers);
- types of institution (phase, type of governance);
- gender;
- social background of intake.

There are, of course, a myriad of other factors that might be examined or compared in this way, and matrices will need to be developed that are relevant to the aims of each study.

Interpreting the data

In this final stage of the process you will attempt to use the process of analysis to make decisions about what is important and what you have found out from your research. This process will also inform the final write-up of your report, and involve the first stages of making decisions about synthesizing and summarizing the data and which quotations or pieces of data to include in the report to elucidate your findings and recommendations.

At this point you may wish to manage the process by utilizing a coding cover sheet for each piece of data, such as an individual transcript similar to the one below in Figure 12.2, (on which is noted the main themes that have been identified with a further space for notes on content that will serve to enable the first processes in analysis).

Respondent code/pseudonym:	
Thematic Coding	Content Analysis
Primary theme/code	
Secondary themes/code	
1.	
2.	
3.	
4.	

Figure 12.2   Coding cover sheet

The importance of returning to research questions

The overarching aim of any research project is to seek answers to the questions posed and the aims stated. In most cases, at least initially, it is those questions or research aims that provide some of the key concepts around which data collection will be constructed. However, as noted earlier, it is possible that new and unexpected concepts will emerge that will be relevant to the focus of the research, and will therefore have to be taken into account in the overall analysis and interpretation of data. The organization of the analysis will tend to be most effective where the initial research questions, posed in the introduction to the study, are employed as the structural device. In this way data from the various sources, both in terms of research populations (and sub-populations) and research tools, are combined in order to address each question in turn. Once the data you have collected have been analyzed, these then need to be brought into contact with both the theoretical models and perspectives, appropriate to the focus of the study, and the outcomes of published research, which will already have been analyzed in your review of the literature (Burton et al., 2008).

One of the main benefits of qualitative research is that it provides depth in terms of research analysis and findings. This is because qualitative data come in the form of material that is rich in meaning and can be analyzed in variety of ways to draw out significance and cultural resonances. For example, a one-hour interview may take several hours to transcribe and is likely to contain around 10,000 words of dialogue, including the main points of the argument, assertions, facts, reflections, contentions, and so on. Since a single research project may involve 10, 20, 50 interviews or more as well as other forms of data-gathering, it is not infrequent for qualitative researchers to feel they are being overwhelmed by a deluge of data. In other words, 'overload is a constant danger' (Robson, 2002: 456), one which frequently leads to a phrase commonly employed by many qualitative researchers – which is 'drowning in data'.

In this situation it will be helpful to return to the original research question and objectives to see whether they can provide you with an initial impetus in the identification of key categories and will thereby restore some order to this data chaos. Many professional qualitative researchers employ specialist software packages such as NUD*IST and NVivo, which can provide useful tools for the systematic storage and retrieval of data and thus manage the process of analysis in a less painful and more manageable way.

Data analysis is a complex and intricate process which involves more than simply sorting information items and proceeds in a non-linear and unpredictable manner. In this sense it is to be perceived as a continuous dialogue that takes place between the data itself, pre-determined and emergent codes, relevant practical and theoretical perspectives (including government frameworks and the research literature), and last but not least, a researcher's own professional practice knowledge (Burton et al., 2008).

Challenges in data analysis

As we have already established, data analysis consists of a number of strategies which involve the filtering, linking and distilling of a diverse body of information. All three processes serve to identify data that are related to the focus of the study and respond to the research questions/objectives. Whilst the filtering or 'reduction of data' (Gray, 2004: 321) through constant comparison with the research objectives and tentative propositions aims to achieve succinctness and a coherence to findings, *triangulation* is used to enhance the validity of outcomes. This can be achieved by combining various data sources, perspectives, settings, times and methods, and looking for convergent messages, thereby strengthening the validity of a claim. As with every investigation the ultimate goal is to tell a story (Wolcott, 1994); however this involves more than simply listing a collection of data. By identifying emerging patterns or trends we can explore potential linkages in our endeavour to understand and explain the underlying reasons for certain phenomena. Analysis could thus be conceived as a dialogue that takes place between the description and interpretation of data, or as a mutually interdependent process where analysis informs interpretation and vice versa (Burton et al., 2008). As mentioned earlier, the relevant literature forms an integral part of this process. This view resonates with Strauss and Corbin who believe that:

> ... the interplay of reading the literature and doing an analysis of it, then moving out into the field to verify it against the reality can yield an integrated picture and enhance the conceptual richness of the theory. (1990: 55)

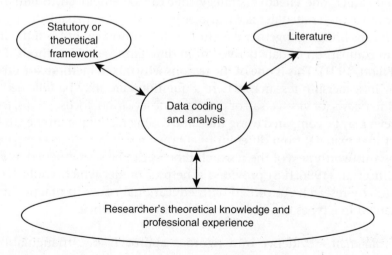

Figure 12.3   The dialogical process of data analysis

Particularly where the emergence of new codes is concerned, making reference to the research literature can enhance their validity, while further reading can result in the discovery of new, relevant codes which hitherto have not been included in the analysis. In addition, it is commonly accepted as good practice to involve more than one researcher in the analysis of data, as it can provide further perspectives (another form of triangulation) and an element of consistency with the aim of enhancing the validity of outcomes and the trustworthiness of the research. One method of overcoming the challenges in data analysis that is especially relevant in leadership research is shown in Figure 12.3, which shows a model based on the idea that the researcher should operate in a 'dialogic' manner within which the process of data coding and analysis involves constant reference back to the statutory or theoretical framework, the concepts in the literature, and the researcher's theoretical and professional knowledge.

Validity, reliability and trustworthiness

The concepts of validity and reliability were discussed in some detail in Chapter 3, but it is important to note that these are especially problematic in relation to qualitative research. As we have already pointed out, validity and reliability are complex terms with multi-layered meanings, but in general can be defined as follows:

> *Validity* is the extent to which a text, experiment, or piece of research actually measures what it set out to measure.
> *Reliability* is the degree to which the measure of a concept is stable and consistent over time between different but similar samples and projects.

As noted earlier, one effective strategy that can be employed to enhance the validity of research outcomes is the use of processes which enable triangulation which means bringing together data from different sources or from the integration and comparison of data derived from different research methods (Denzin, 1970; Elliott, 1991). This is one of the reasons why mixed methods are especially popular in leadership research, where a questionnaire may be followed by in-depth interviews (or vice-versa); or data from observation, focus groups, logs and interviews may be compared using the same coding technique. In the latter case, the fact that material from different qualitative research tools is compared and that the trustworthiness of the research process can be strengthened, is vital.

McNiff et al. (1996:108) provided a helpful model which could be transferred to any research concerned with educational issues in practice settings. It presented five types of validation by a critical audience:

- *Self-validation* – evidence in a rigorous approach (e.g. triangulation, the piloting of tools).
- *Peer validation* – feedback from practitioners in the field.

- *Up-liner validation* – a positive evaluation of research outcomes by those in authority.
- *Client validation* – improvement of the service.
- *Academic validation* – feedback from a tutor/mentor in higher education.

In traditional research, validity, reliability and generalizability constitute the essential quality criteria, the latter two of which are difficult, if not well-nigh impossible, to fulfil by qualitative researchers undertaking small-scale investigations within their own practice setting. Whilst quantitative data analysis makes use of statistical procedures that lend themselves to enhancing the validity, reliability and generalizability of research findings in a scientific/ positivistic sense, qualitative researchers undertaking small-scale investigations in their own practice setting will frequently employ alternative quality criteria. In order to make such claims the sample that is used needs to be fully representative of the population as a whole (Bryman, 1988: 35), and while the qualitative researcher may try to develop a sample that reflects broadly the main characteristics of the group under study, it is rare that a claim can be made that the sample is fully representative, thus introducing a series of biases. Since, by its nature, qualitative research is not susceptible to, or at least is not usually subject to, statistical techniques which attempt to account for the nature of the sample, claims for generalizability and reliability beyond the research setting are problematic if not impossible. Similar problems also arise with regard to fulfilling the criterion of reliability, which refers to the degree of consistency with which instances are assigned to the same category by different observers or by the same observer on different occasions (Hammersley, 1992: 67).

Consequently, qualitative analysis has to defend itself against claims of subjectivity, or accept that subjectivity is an inevitable element within the research process as a whole, and the analytical process in particular. In this respect it is helpful to refer to Bassey (1999), whose notions of *trustworthiness* are deemed more appropriate where notions of generalizability are put to one side and substituted with more appropriate terms that suggest the researcher will at least try to make the process of research consistent within the defined parameters of the individual project. Whilst the validity value will be largely determined by the extent to which the findings are directly related to the issues or problems identified at the outset of the research process, and how well they respond to the research questions posed, its trustworthiness is reflected in the selection of appropriate methods and how systematically they have been employed (Burton et al., 2008).

The main thing a qualitative researcher must keep in mind in the process of analysis is the extent to which the data generated answer the research question or questions, and this will rely to a large extent on the appropriate selection of data collection tools and the development and employment of appropriate analytical processes.

Summary ☐

The analysis of qualitative data can be a complex and problematic process. It takes time and effort for a researcher to become completely familiar with the data as well as care, and often some degree of creativity, or at least flexibility, in order to code, categorize, and finally interpret the data. This process cannot be rushed, and each project is likely to require the development of specific tools for analysis such as special matrices or coding sheets. The process can be enhanced by the use of electronic data analysis packages but, in essence, such means replicate and electronically systematize exactly the same processes that are undertaken when manual analysis takes place. Whilst qualitative research can rarely, if ever, claim to offer generalizable universal truths, it can offer rich interpretations and insights that may be of vital importance in institutional development and change. For this reason alone, anyone undertaking leadership research would be unwise to neglect such approaches.

Further reading

Drever, E. (1995) *Using Semi-Structured Interview in Small-Scale Research.* Edinburgh: Scottish Council for Educational Research.

Saldana, J. (2013) *The Coding Manual for Qualitative Researchers.* London: Sage.

Silverman, D. (2001) *Interpreting Qualitative Data: Methods For Analysing Talk, Text and Interaction.* London: Sage.

Silverman, D. (2004) *Qualitative Research: Theory, Method and Practice.* London: Sage.

Symon, G. and Cassell, C. (eds) (1998) *Qualitative Methods and Analysis in Organisational Research: A Practical Guide.* London: Sage.

13

The Uses of Leadership Research

Aims

In this chapter we will be considering some of the most important uses of leadership research. Leadership research has been identified as one of the four main building blocks of the field of educational leadership and management (see Bush, 2010a), with the remaining three blocks being practice, theory and policy. It is clear that the outcomes of leadership research may have profound influences upon these latter three blocks. Colleagues engaged in leadership research continue to report that research is about finding something out and producing new knowledge. In this chapter we focus upon knowledge production and the learning journey that may accrue for individuals who engage in leadership research. We aim to enable practitioners, students, and others undertaking research to reflect upon their experience and necessary learning and identify the personal transformation and professional development that has taken place. We include a section on knowledge generation in relation to theory and theorizing, and aim to enable you to consider your leadership research in relation to practice, theory and policy. In a final section we explore the leadership research agenda in relation to the international focus upon the improvement and effectiveness of educational organizations. In so doing, we aim to firmly root the use of leadership research in advancing the enactment of educational leadership itself. Finally, a list of suggested further reading is included at the end of the chapter to enable you to explore items of interest, and establish for yourself the breadth of audience your research might touch as well as the current research areas that are of particular interest both in the United Kingdom and internationally. By the end of this chapter you should be able to:

- understand the relevance of leadership research;
- defend the use of research in personal and professional development;
- see how research contributes to practice, theory and policy;
- make connections between leadership research and educational improvement and effectiveness.

The relevance of leadership research

Some years ago Hammersley (1993b) asked what the relevance of educational research was, as few teachers had read it and the contexts in which they worked were so variable that any one piece of research could hardly apply in every situation. In this chapter we aim to establish some of the key areas in educational research by exploring its relationship to practice, theory and policy. Assuming that research can make a difference to those who use it to inform practice, theory and policy, it has been suggested that knowledge generation by research should advance in a 'systematic and critical way' (see Bassey, 1999) in order that the carefully achieved outcomes of research may add new information to the knowledge base that is credible and trustworthy (see Chapter 3). Credibility and trustworthiness are self-evidently important in enabling researchers and other intended recipients to access and use this new knowledge with confidence in their decision making. Furlong and Oancea (2005) devised criteria for evaluating the extent to which the outcomes of educational research projects would influence practice and policy. They established criteria based around the extent to which educational research could provide practitioners with information to guide their practice and the extent to which research would change those practitioners by enabling them to develop personally. In a later work, Hammersley (2008) suggested that educational research should be judged on its 'potential' to impact upon practice.

All educational research embodies notions of rigour, credibility, and a desire to advance the available knowledge base. For many leadership researchers their end goal is to help inform change which will ultimately improve the experience and success of learners and subsequently enhance the life trajectories of those learners. If we look at the history of educational research (see, for example, De Landsheere, 1993) this reveals not only successes but also some uncertainty and clear differences in the mindset of some teachers and researchers, resulting in a theory-practice divide limiting the use of theory to inform practice. Although the dissemination of leadership research findings is often well addressed through publications, seminars, reports and practitioner-linked agencies, some items of potentially useful research may not reach their intended audience and remain lost in academic journals, perhaps awaiting some future discovery and application. Maxwell (1998) identifies the three purposes of educational research as personal purposes, practical purposes, and research purposes, but not all research is perceived as fulfilling such purposes. Indeed some research within the field of educational leadership and management has been criticized on the grounds that it may lack relevance to the work of educational organizations (Gorard, 2005). Such criticisms are sometimes based upon a perceived 'lack of evidence' in numerical terms for the assertions made. However, much research, it may be argued, (such as that pertaining to, for example, leadership for diversity and leadership for learning) is clearly highly related to the everyday enactment of leadership in educational organizations and such research can make a difference. In this new millennium, notions of knowledge transfer and the importance of establishing the impact of research in relation to intended recipients may serve to diminish claims of lack of relevance to the work of educational organizations. In our view, the outcomes of leadership research have had, and continue to have, some profound influences upon practice, leadership, training, theory, policy and the ongoing research agenda in many parts of the world. Bush (2010) rightly suggests that international interest in educational leadership has never been greater than it is now.

Educationalists as researchers: personal and professional development

Hoyle (1980) distinguishes between those teachers who are primarily interested in practice and those teachers who more actively seek to link theory and practice as a means to learn and hence improve their work. Whilst many teachers may regard research and theory as remote from their daily teaching, Carr and Kemmis (1986) held that teacher engagement in action research could promote critical reflection, enabling those teachers to question the efficacy of established teaching procedures and processes. In 2000, the Department for Education and Employment in the England introduced 'Best Practice Research Scholarships' for teachers (DfEE, 2000) to help promote practitioner research and the benefits that may follow from teacher engagement in research work. The scholarships were only available in relatively small numbers and were eventually withdrawn to be replaced by an initiative to create 'networked learning communities' (NCSL, 2003). This initiative aimed to enable groups of teachers from different schools to meet and share ideas, such as those that emerged from their own investigatory activities, in order that a dialogue and sharing could give rise to improvements in teaching and learning. The value of 'practitioner research' centrally promoted in this way has attracted both protagonists (see Bartlett and Burton, 2006) and also antagonists (see Gorard, 2002). Whilst some commentators see practitioner research activity as being personally and professionally beneficial with possible advantages for learners, others see engagement in academic research as an elite activity requiring extensive training. Practitioner research has also been viewed by its detractors as over descriptive and too concerned with everyday teaching problems at the expense of adding to the wider available knowledge base.

Research training in the United Kingdom and in many other countries can be accessed through doctoral study in the form of a PhD, through a professional doctorate programme such as an EdD, and via Master's Programmes. Bird et al. (2005) advocate that Master's work done by teachers as part of their professional development has significant benefit for the individual and can extend knowledge and skills relatable to the teachers' own professional context. This linkage of theory and practice is promoted in many such Master's programmes. Professional doctorates are offered in a wide variety of countries and generally consist of subject-based input, research training, and the presentation of a piece of original research worthy of publication and able to make a contribution to the existing knowledge base in the field. Professional doctorates involve research and theorizing and have value in informing practice (Bowden, Bourner and Laing, 2002). It has also been suggested that professional doctorates are underpinned by a desire to transform practice (Scott et al., 2004). Notwithstanding the need to maintain a firm rooting in professional practice, engagement with a professional doctorate requires participants to adopt a new identity: they need to become educational researchers. Scott and Morrison (2010) point to the potential difficulties in identity change that can be encountered as experienced educational practitioners seek to become educational researchers at doctoral level:

> During the various rites of passage from competent professional, to novice doctoral initiate, through to finally achieving doctoral status at the convocation ceremony, 'schizophrenic' tendencies are averted for some students by the compartmentalisation of identities whilst at university and in professional employment – one being academic and the other professional. (Scott and Morrison, 2010: 25)

Practitioners participating in doctoral, and to some extent Master's, research training are likely to need to reconcile the cultural differences between the world of practice and the world of the educational researcher. This can present challenges but also opportunities for further development both personally and professionally. In a study conducted in the United States to explore the transformation of educational practitioners into educational researchers, various potential difficulties were identified as individuals were asked to readdress their cultural orientation from normative to analytic, personal to intellectual, particular to universal, and experiential to theoretical (Labaree, 2003). Despite these potential difficulties, a study in England conducted by Pilkington (2009) established that the motivation to undertake a professional doctorate programme was strongly related to a participant's desire for self-development and a desire to improve outcomes for their learners. This author emphasizes the necessity of careful academic integration of such participants and advocates the need to build up their confidence as beginning researchers in an academic community.

The academic and research socialization processes for doctoral researchers (see Gardner, 2007, 2009) and the influence of research supervision and pedagogy on their learning (see Johnson et al., 2000; Gatfield, 2005; Hockey and Allen-Collinson, 2005; Petersen, 2007; Zhao, Golde and McCormick, 2007; Lee, 2008; Mainhard, van der Rijst and Wubbels, 2009; Hopwood, 2010; Martinsuo and Turkulainen, 2011) have received much international attention. How such participants come to see themselves and the world differently, if indeed they do, is likely to be mediated by the learning environment they experience and by participant factors such as gender, stage of transition to becoming a researcher, nationality, and mode of part-time or full-time study. In an exploration of doctoral learning journeys, Wisker et al. (2010) report the occurrence of 'learning leaps' as new conceptual levels of understanding are reached. These authors describe challenges to the security of the participant's 'self' and deepening knowledge as important in achieving such learning leaps. Influential in participant personal and professional development at this level is the opportunity to experience meta-learning, in other words, to take the opportunity to become truly aware of one's own learning and take control of it (see Biggs, 1985; Meyer and Shanahan, 2004). In summary, a potentially important use of leadership research is to enable the personal and professional development of those who come to engage in it through advancing their learning empowerment.

Knowledge generation: a contribution to practice, theory and policy

The research literature reveals many authors who have concerned themselves with exploring knowledge generation and how such knowledge generation may contribute to practice, theory and policy. For example, Wallace and Poulson (2003) describe five types of 'intellectual project' which may be undertaken in order to develop theoretical and research knowledge that is of relevance to practice and policy. 'Knowledge-for-understanding' may be sought in order to achieve better levels of insight rather than directly seeking to improving practice or policy. 'Knowledge-for-critical-evaluation' may be sought in order to critically examine the ideologies lying beneath practice and policy. 'Knowledge-for-action' may be sought to inform direct improvement with respect to practice and policy. Wallace and Poulson suggest that 'instrumentalism' is concerned with attempts to impart practice knowledge and 'reflexive action' is concerned with research which attempts to develop, improve and share practice knowledge from a self-critical standpoint. In all cases, it is shown that particular foci of research have the potential to inform either policy, or practice, or both.

The work of Ribbins and Gunter (2002) and Gunter and Ribbins (2003) ascribes leadership research work to five different knowledge domains. Each domain points the reader towards a different approach and the type of questions that might be asked and addressed:

- *Conceptual research* 'is concerned with issues of ontology and epistemology and with conceptual clarification'. For example, what does leadership mean?
- *Humanistic research* 'seeks to gather and theorize from the experiences and biographies of those who are leaders and those who are led'. For example,

how have you learned from the leadership of heads you have worked with or worked for?

- *Critical research* 'is concerned to reveal, and emancipate practitioners from the various forms of social injustice and the oppression of established but unjustifiable structures and processes of power'. For example, to what extent do you share your power and distribute your leadership?
- *Evaluative research* 'may be taken to mean any research that seeks to abstract and measure impact, in this case of leadership and its effectiveness at -micro, -meso and -macro levels of social interaction'. For example, how do you measure the impact of your leadership on teaching, learning and examination results?
- *Instrumental research* 'seeks to provide leaders and others with effective strategies and tactics to deliver organizational and system-level goals'. For example, which strategies and tactics that you have used in developing a successful school would you like to share with your colleagues?

Research knowledge has been viewed by many as essential in informing and criticizing policy development and policy implementation at local, national and international levels. For example, Ball (2011) identifies new research questions which need to be addressed by educational policy and leadership researchers given the advent of new sorts of providers and sponsors entering the maintained education sector in the United Kingdom. Ball also identifies potential tensions between national education policy interests and international company financial interests. In a similar critical vein, Hartley (2007, 2010) points to the national promotion of leadership distribution in schools and colleges in the United Kingdom when there is a dearth of empirical evidence that distributing leadership has any direct positive effect on learner outcomes at all. He argues that this is a case of policy formation in advance of research evidence.

It is also evident from the research literature that research has a strong relationship with theory. For example, theory may be used to inform a research study or used to explain and interpret research findings and so generate new knowledge and new understanding. A theory may be thought of as an expression of collected knowledge or a collection of ideas that give coherence and meaning to thinking and research outcomes. Wallace and Poulson (2003) suggest that:

> Theories are widely viewed as a coherent system of connected concepts, sometimes lying within one or more perspectives. They may be used to describe, interpret, explain or, more normatively, to prescribe what should be done to improve an aspect of the social world, as in a progressive theory of education. (2003:13)

Thomas and James (2006) distinguish between two kinds of theory: firstly, theory that provides tools for thinking and which serves to map out a problem area, and secondly, theory as explanation and prediction which can be proved or disproved by empirical investigation as found in the natural sciences. Davies (1999) distinguishes between six types of theoretical activity:

- *Descriptive* i.e. theory about what people, institutions or societies actually do, or say, or are.
- *Explanatory* i.e. theory that asserts why people, institutions or societies do, say, or are certain things.
- *Conceptual* i.e. theory by which we map our world by imposing new concepts, ideas and categories upon it.
- *Prescriptive* i.e. theory which contains explicitly or implicitly, what ought to be or what should be.
- *Predictive* i.e. theory that can be tested.
- *Interpretive* i.e. theory that seeks to describe and conceptualize often high levels of complexity.

There is no single theory of leadership and management in education and such a theory would be highly unlikely given the wide variety of contexts in which educational leadership and management takes place (Bush, 2011). As previously mentioned, the relationship between theory and practice is not secure in the minds of some educationalists and some researchers, and the theory-practice divide in education and in leadership and management studies still exists (English, 2002; Bush, 2011). This is a pity given that theory may serve to explain and inform practice and also provide a basis upon which to better inform educational leadership and management actions. If unifying theories could be established they have the potential to bring together the key tenets needed to inform development activities within educational organizations. At the same time, unifying theories would have the potential to diminish the need, despite differences in context, to re-invent the same solutions over and over again in individual organizations. In summary, an important use of leadership research is to generate knowledge pertinent to the understanding and advancement of practice, theory and policy within national and international education systems.

Leadership research and educational improvement and effectiveness

Research on school effectiveness and school improvement has shown that the two main factors influencing the quality of education are classroom practice and the quality of leadership (Leithwood et al., 2007). Rhodes and Bisschoff (2012) suggest that despite the many challenges facing leaders, leadership and the effective school are related via strategy and vision, understanding and developing people, fostering enabling cultures, communication, managing the teaching and learning programme, and helping to balance bureaucracy with passion. Wrigley (2008) reminds us that in our search for improvement we should not lose sight of the kind of future we would like to create and those who will be the beneficiaries of any changes proposed. Although policy and socio-economic and cultural differences at a local, national and international level will be influential in perceptions of the role of educational leadership, many studies have contributed to a firm belief that good leaders are instrumental in establishing good schools (see, for example, Teddlie and Reynolds, 2000; Hallinger and Snidvongs, 2005; Muijs, 2006). In short, the relationship between leadership research and institutional development has been established over many years, and a firm belief has grown up that good leadership is linked to educational effectiveness and that good leaders are necessary for educational improvements to occur.

We hold that research activity serves to establish and elaborate the key tenets surrounding our present understandings of the empirical agenda for leadership and educational improvement, and it also prompts further consideration of advancement in the future. In both national and international contexts a number of important research agendas continue to attract much interest from the leadership research community. For example, educational improvement based upon leadership for inclusion, equity and diversity (Bush, 2009; Lumby, 2010), a rapidly growing research focus on leadership development as a key component of school improvement (Bush, 2008), models and approaches to leadership such as leadership distribution (Spillane, 2006; Harris, 2009), and leadership for learning (MacBeath and Dempster, 2009; Rhodes and Brundrett, 2010) may be included. Additionally, the initiation and success of change events in establishing and sustaining improvement have frequently been linked to leadership (Wallace, 2002; Hallinger and Snidvongs, 2005; Hargreaves and Fink, 2006; PricewaterhouseCoopers, 2007) and continue to draw much research interest. In summary, a crucial use of leadership research is in the establishment of contemporary insights so that local, national and international audiences may reflect critically upon their own work and activities. Specifically, it has a key role in providing new knowledge which can be used directly or indirectly to inform practice, theory and policy, and thereby enable improvements to occur.

Summary ☐

Educational research, including leadership research, has over many years generated new knowledge which has informed a variety of audiences. This chapter elaborated on three vital uses of leadership research in its focus upon 'personal and professional development', 'practice, theory and policy', and 'educational improvement and effectiveness' respectively. Whether adopting quantitative, qualitative or mixed-methods approaches, leadership researchers have been successful in advancing the field both nationally and internationally. Leadership is often framed as a social interaction in which those with power, authority, influence and sufficient people-skills can work with others to offer inspiration and secure their followership. The enactment of high quality leadership is rightly acknowledged as an essential component within educational systems and beyond. Overall, the chapter established agreement with Maxwell's (1998) analysis that research has key uses in personal and practical development and in advancing a continued research agenda. The chapter also advocated that leadership research, as Bush (2010a) rightly suggests, is one of the four main building blocks of the field of educational leadership and management, and demonstrated unequivocal relationships between leadership research and practice, theory and policy, which Bush (2010a) rightly identifies as the three other major building blocks of the field. It was concluded that leadership research can and does make a difference in the lives and experiences of all those involved within the educational field of endeavour.

Further reading

Brundrett, M. and Rhodes, C.P. (2010) *Leadership for Quality and Accountability in Education*. London: Routledge.

Bush, T., Bell, L. and Middlewood (eds) (2010) *The Principles of Educational Leadership and Management* (2nd edition). London: Sage.

Dimmock, C. (2011) *Leadership, Capacity Building and School Improvement: Concepts, Themes and Impact*. London: Routledge.

Northouse, P.G. (2006) *Leadership: Theory and Practice* (4th edition). London: Sage.

Western, S. (2007) *Leadership: A Critical Text*. London: Sage.

Williams, C. (2012) *Researching Power, Elites and Leadership*. London: Sage.

14

Conclusion: Writing Reports and Making Sense of Outcomes

Aims

This chapter will focus on revealing the ways in which a research project may be reported in order to ensure lucid, comprehensible and unambiguous final research outcomes and recommendations. The differing approaches to structuring research reports, including dissertations and theses, will also be explored. Central to this argument will be the concept that as a researcher you should, from the outset of a project, analyze how you intend to develop the overall structure of your investigation so that this can be reflected in the final outcomes of your research findings. By the end of this chapter you should be able to:

- appreciate the importance of structuring your research report in a manner that is fit for purpose;
- be able to maintain a consistency between the purposes and the research outcomes;
- understand the importance of basic skills in scholarship, and especially the skills involved in referencing appropriately;
- be aware of the ways in which reports should be adjusted to meet the needs of non-specialist audiences;
- be aware of the role of research in influencing leadership practice.

Researching educational leadership

This book set out to provide an examination of the need to relate research to leadership in education. The overriding aim that underpinned its conception was to engage with new ideas and research findings by testing new practices and evaluating change through enhanced and formalized reflection. To this end we have attempted to assist in understanding how research can be used to inform and improve practice; in seeing the value of embedding and evaluating initiatives; and in appreciating the value of educational research processes to leaders and researchers.

Deciding how to present and write a research report needs to be as central to your research project as the methodology itself (Thody, 2006: 17). It is essential that research reports should be clear, well-structured pieces of work that 'hold together' well. There are, however, several factors that will militate against you achieving such structural integrity in your work:

- Research study is often undertaken in a fractured, interrupted manner, especially when undertaken as a practitioner rather than as a postgraduate student or professional researcher.
- Your literature review may be wide-ranging and could therefore have a tendency to seem diffuse if the material is not integrated well.
- Your methodology may adopt an integrative stance that employs blended approaches to research which may seem difficult to manage.
- The data you derive from different research tools or different cases may seem problematic to assimilate.
- You may find it difficult to integrate the different elements of the conceptual statement, review, methodology and analysis.

Because of these various factors you will need to develop a logical method for structuring your final report or the danger will exist that your ideas may seem incoherent and your recommendations will be ignored.

Developing a logical structure in research reports

Throughout this book we have recommended a rational approach to research which has emphasized the identification of researchable problems, the creation of clear research questions and associated aims, and the construction of a research methodology designed to address the research topic in the most productive way. This rational process extends to the final outputs of the research project since clear problems and carefully crafted aims can, ideally at least, result in you producing a seamless research report. Constructing an appropriate structure for your research project is vital from the outset because it will facilitate:

- clarity in your conceptualization of the research;
- lucidity in the research process;
- precision in your analysis of data;
- structural integrity in your final research report or thesis.

This approach will assist you in your final writing of the research report, since all of the elements of this logical approach will feed into your account of what happened in the research process. Such reports can be complex and challenging to write because they contain within them a number of ambiguities and contradictions. Because of these issues you will need to tell the 'story' of your research in a way which will engage readers but allow the report to remain analytical in nature. Your research should help to create new understandings and create new knowledge, but it should also synthesize previous research findings and theoretical perspectives, and you will need to show that you have mastered the theory as well as shown the practical implications of your findings. However, the paramount challenge here is often the necessity to provide a sense of 'narrative flow' whilst ensuring structural integrity within the work (Burton et al., 2008). This is because the potentially disjointed nature of a dissertation, thesis or report will tend to make the creation of essential linkages between sections seem more problematic.

Note that most dissertations, theses and reports in the field of educational research will follow the standard structure of:

- abstract;
- introduction;
- literature review;
- methodology;
- data presentation and analysis;
- conclusion;
- references;
- appendices.

This structure can, however, be varied slightly or even significantly if you feel this is appropriate and if the agency or institution to which you are reporting allows or requires such variance. For instance, data presentation and data analysis is often separated into two sections, and the literature review may well be further subdivided into a number of chapters rather than one monolithic and sometimes dominant section. To some extent such a decision will depend on pragmatic issues such as the allowed length of the report and the purpose which it serves. So, a brief report to professional colleagues or other stakeholders in an institution may only contain a short outline of the background context rather than an in-depth analysis of the literature, and only a very general outline of the research approach to show that the work has been carried out in order to lead to conclusions and recommendations for amended practice. Equally, a Master's dissertation may adopt the whole of the structure above but is unlikely to allow sufficient room for many subdivisions. Finally a PhD thesis may well be further subdivided since the volume of material would be too great to accommodate in so few major sub-sections without the danger of overburdening the reader on a particular topic.

Nonetheless, the sections outlined above are those most frequently included since they provide an opportunity to explore all of the key elements that make up a research study. There are a number of ways to provide an underpinning device that will act as a thread throughout these sections. In essence, all such approaches can be distilled into the idea that the fundamental themes that emerge from the research questions should reappear in each section or chapter. Figure 14.1 outlines in more detail the structure of a research report by suggesting which items should appear in each section.

The Introduction should:
Present the topic.
Present the macro and micro issues that make the topic relevant and important.
Make a claim to originality for the research.
Present and justify the overall research questions/issues.
Present and justify the research sub-questions/aims/issues.

The Literature Review should:
Summarize the key literature, in depth, on the topic that you have chosen.
Address, in detail, the sub-questions or research aims that you have set yourself.
Present a coherent line of argument about the topic under scrutiny.

The Methodology section should:
Present and justify the methodological approach that you have employed.
Include a clear, straightforward and unambiguous outline of the methods you have employed in terms of the sample, tools, and methods of analysis.
Address key, standard methodological issues such as validity, reliability, ethical considerations, etc.
Address, where appropriate, the issues associated with being an 'insider researcher' (especially when undertaking a case study of one's own institution).

Data presentation and analysis should:
Be structured in accordance with one of three main approaches to presenting and analyzing data. These include:

According to research questions/ issues.
According to research tools.
According to cases.

The Conclusion should:
Reiterate the overall topic and the reasons for the investigation.
State the key findings.
Present or represent any 'model' or 'models' that may have been developed.
Suggest any further research that might be pursued.
Outline any inadequacies in the research.
Provide a final statement that may indicate the importance and originality of the research and its potential 'impact' on practice.

Figure 14.1   The structure of a research report

As this figure implies, general convention dictates the overall structure of the report but there is no 'proper' or universally agreed method of creating a substructure for these larger sections. However, the most common, and frequently the most successful, method of structuring the smaller elements that make up a report is to employ an iterative process that develops the themes derived from the original research questions. Thus, in the ideal report, your Introduction would 'set the scene' by outlining the macro context (such as government reports, legislation or other initiatives), and the micro context of the institution or institutions within which the research is situated. You will, in essence, be making a clear argument for the relevance of the research and perhaps also some claim for its originality, which can either be through arguing that the area explored is in some way unmapped territory, or that the context within which the research is operating has not been explored fully in relation to the issue, or even that the methodology employed has been brought to bear on the topic and so may cast some new light on the issue.

Crucially, it is customary that you must state and justify the research questions or issues that form the basis of your research. These questions will embody themes that you can then utilize to underpin the rest of the document. So, for instance, if five major themes emerge in the research questions, these same five themes may form the sub-sections of the Literature Review that will be the succeeding section of your report. The Methodology section is, to some extent at least, an aside from the ongoing threads of the study, since its function is to explain and justify the research methods adopted, to make claims for generalizability (if appropriate), and to assure the reader that proper ethical procedures have been carried out. Nonetheless, this section will still reflect the thematic elements of the research since the methodology employed, the tools used, the sample constructed, and the location of the research will all be dictated by the issues that you wish to explore and it is vital to be able to show the ways in which your research approach was designed to address the research goals that you set for yourself. The overarching themes will re-emerge with greater clarity in the subsequent Data Presentation and Analysis sections where these may be used as devices to report on the research, often in the form of sub-sections. The thematic approach will reach its denouement in the Conclusion since it will be inevitable that you will want to return to the issues stated right at the start of the study in order to summarize what you have discovered, what the recommendations for changes to practice are, and what further research might be undertaken.

Scholarly skills: referencing

Any formal research report should reveal that the researcher has high levels of skill and understanding in scholarship and scholarly conventions. This will include such matters as using appropriate conventions in terms of Abstracts, Contents Pages, Lists of Figures, the overall structure and presentation of the document, and the use of conventional spelling. One of the most important sets of skills to demonstrate is that associated with the appropriate referencing of material in the text of the report. Most research reports in the social sciences

Collecting material for referencing

For *books*, record:

The author's or editor's name (or names)
The year the book was published (bracketed)
The title of the book (italicised)
If it is an edition other than the first
The city the book was published in
The name of the publisher

For *journal articles* record:

The author's name or names
The year in which the journal was published
The title of the article
The title of the journal (italicized)
The page number/s of the article in the journal
As much other information as you can find about the journal, for example the volume and issue numbers

For *electronic resources*, try to collect the information as above if it is available, but also record:

The date you accessed the source
The electronic address or email
The type of electronic resource (email, discussion forum, WWW page, etc.)
In addition to these details, when you are taking notes, if you copy direct quotations or if you put the author's ideas in your own words, write down the page numbers you got the information from.

References or Bibliography

When you use the Harvard System, you are only usually required to produce a reference list – i.e. all the sources you have referred to in the text. However, you may also want you to produce a bibliography where you list *all* the sources you have consulted, but not referred to, in the text.

How to list references in a reference list

Book with one author
Brundrett, M. (2000) *Beyond Competence: The Challenge for Educational Management.* King's Lynn: Peter Francis Publishing.

Book with two authors
Burton, N. and Brundrett, M. (2005) *Leading the Curriculum in the Primary School.* London: Sage.

Book with three or more authors
Burton, N., Brundrett, M. and Jones, M. (2008) *Doing Your Research Project: Research Skills for the Educational Practitioner.* London: Sage

Book with an editor
Brundrett, M. (ed.) (2012) *Principles of School Leadership* (2nd edition). London: Sage.

Chapter in a book written by someone other than the editor
Rhodes, C. and Brundrett, M. (2010) 'Leadership for learning', in T. Bush and L. Bell (eds), *The Principles of Educational Leadership and Management* (2nd edition). London: Sage.

Journal articles
Rhodes, C. and Brundrett, M. (2012) Retaining leadership talent in schools, *International Studies in Educational Administration*, 40 (1): 19–34.

Web pages
DfEE (2001) *Supporting the Target Setting Process.* London: DfEE. Accessed at www.standards.dfes.gov.uk/ts/pdf/DfES_065_2001.pdf (last accessed 20 August 2007).

Figure 14.2   The Harvard Referencing System

will employ the Harvard referencing system as outlined in Figure 14.2. However, you need to note here that there are a number of other systems for referencing, and requirements may vary from institution to institution, and so as a researcher you would always be well advised to check on which particular system has been adopted.

There are also a number of electronic systems, already referred to in Chapter 4, such as *EndNote*, which will help you to manage references, and if used properly these can simplify the process greatly and allow you to present references in a variety of different formats without the intense labour required in manually reorganizing the material.

Professional reports to non-specialist audiences

As noted earlier in this chapter, practitioner researchers may wish, or be required, to provide a report to a non-specialist audience such as a governing body, a student committee, a governors' sub-committee, a parents committee, or the like. With such an audience the structural conventions that underpin the more formal method of report writing embodied in a dissertation or thesis may need to be modified to take account of the level of expertise of the readers. Inevitably, such reports are likely to be much shorter than a thesis or report to a funding agency and indeed may only contain a few hundred words. Detail may be left out in an attempt to convey key findings, references may be excluded altogether, and much of the complex reasoning that goes into a meth-odology section may be deemed inappropriate. Nonetheless, it is important not to patronise such an audience, and the same essential structure of context, main aims, previous perspectives, main approach to the research, and main findings can be used to powerful and persuasive effect. One simple method of conveying central messages swiftly is to provide an *Executive Summary* in the form of a few main bullet points at the start of the report. This approach, often combined with a very clear set of *Conclusions and Recommendations*, can be very effective in leading to agreement on changes in practice. Indeed, it is this issue of developing and improving practice that is crucial to many leadership researchers and it is to this topic that we turn to next.

Using research outcomes to inform practice

Practitioner research can provide a formidable toolkit for analyzing the complex social situations that obtain in classrooms in order to influence school strategy and target setting (Burton et al., 2008). This is nowhere more true than in the field of leadership research where the leader, at what-ever level, can have considerable influence on the department or organiza-tion that they manage. The highly influential work of Fullan (1993; 1999; 2003) argues that the increasingly diverse nature of societies, the revolution in communications technologies, and new attitudes to learning, have ensured that complexity and change are an unavoidable part of life for those involved in education. We are also aware that managing change can be one of the most challenging elements of any leader's role, and that it is important to try to insert a rational model on to the frequently disordered and fluctuating circumstances that educationalists find themselves in if sustainable and successful change is to be enacted (Morrison, 1998: 13). The best models of change integrate these issues of complexity, moral purpose and the need for sustained and embedded improvement by suggesting that organizational change in education is based on a number of key factors that echo throughout this book and include: the engagement of parents, student and community resources; access to new ideas; a professional community; internalizing the responsibility for change; and, strategic educational planning (Bryk et al., quoted in Fullan, 1999: 35). Well-structured research enables a leader to analyze the complex social context of schools and so influence strategy in a way that would be far more difficult without defensible conclusions based in clear evidence, otherwise colleagues may view any proposed alteration to custom as being simply a bureaucratic exercise based on the whim of an individual manager (Brundrett and Terrell, 2004). The approach outlined in this book, and the ordered, structured and systematic approach to reporting research outlined in this chapter, are designed to avoid such false and often dangerous assumptions.

Summary and final conclusion   ☐

Research has revealed that there is strong evidence of an increasing willingness to support the notion of teaching as an evidence-based profession (Burton and Bartlett, 2005: 182). This is to be applauded, and leaders at all levels in educational institutions should seek to involve themselves with the process and outcomes of research into leadership practice so that they can help to impact positively on student outcomes. Throughout this book we have argued that by establishing the links between leadership practice and research processes, leadership practitioners will be able to more effectively develop the skills that are required to develop our educational institutions in a way which values staff and students and enhances the life chances of those in their charge.

If such research is to achieve these desirable outcomes it is essential that sound questions are formulated and that robust methods are used in order to provide convincing evidence of the need for development and change. We hope that this text has provided both practising and aspiring leadership researchers with some of the knowledge and techniques needed to achieve such clarity.

Further reading

Denscombe, M. (2010) *The Good Research Guide* (4th edition). Maidenhead: Open University Press.

Glatthorn, A.A. and Joyner, R.L. (2005) *Writing the Winning Thesis or Dissertation: A Step-by-Step Guide.* New York: Corwin.

Punch, K.F. (2005) *Introduction to Social Science Research: Quantitative and Qualitative Approaches* (2nd edition). London: Sage.

Wallwork, A. (2011) *English for Writing Research Papers.* New York: Springer.

Weyers, J. and McMillan, K. (2011) *How to Write Dissertations and Project Reports.* London: Prentice-Hall.

Bibliography

Adelman, C., Kemmis, S. and Jenkins, D. (1980) 'Rethinking case study', in H. Simons (ed.), *Towards a Science of the Singular*. Norwich: Centre for Applied Research in Education, University of East Anglia.

Ball, S.J. (1990) Self-doubt and soft data: social and technical trajectories in ethnographic fieldwork, *International Journal of Qualitative Studies in Education*, 3(2): 157–71.

Ball, S.J. (1993) 'Self-doubt and soft data: social and technical trajectories in ethnographic fieldwork', in M. Hammersley (ed.), *Educational Research: Current Issues*. London: Paul Chapman.

Ball, S.J. (2011) A new research agenda for educational leadership and policy, *Management in Education*, 25(2): 50–2.

Barker, D.M. and Rossi, A. (2011) Understanding teachers: the potential and possibility of discourse analysis, *Sport, Education and Society*, 16(2): 139–58.

Bartlett, S. and Burton, D. (2006) Practitioner research or descriptions of classroom practice? A discussion of teachers investigating their classrooms, *Educational Action Research*, 14(3): 395–405.

Bassey, M. (1999) *Case Study in Educational Settings*. Buckingham: Open University Press.

Bassey, M. (2007) 'Case studies', in A. Briggs and M. Coleman (eds), *Research Methods in Educational Leadership and Management* (2nd edition). London: Sage.

Bell, J. (2005) *Doing Your Research Project* (4th edition). Buckingham: Open University Press.

BERA (2011) *Ethical Guidelines for Educational Research*, British Educational Research Association. Available at www.bera.ac.uk (last accessed 16 August 2012).

Beresford, P. (1999) 'Making participation possible: movements of disabled people and psychiatric system survivors', in T. Jordan and A. Lent (eds), *Storming the Millennium: The New Politics of Change*. London: Lawrence & Wishart. pp. 34–50.

Bernard, H.R. (2012) *Social Research Methods: Qualitative and Quantitative Approaches*. Thousand Oaks, CA: Sage.

Biggs, J.B. (1985) The role of metalearning in study processes, *British Journal of Educational Psychology*, 55(3): 185–212.

Bird, M., Ding, S., Hanson, A., Leontovitsch, A. and McCartney, R. (2005) There is nothing as practical as a good theory: an examination of the outcomes of a 'traditional' MA in education for educational professionals, *Journal of In-Service Education*, 31(3): 427–53.

Birley, G. and Moreland, N. (1998) *A Practical Guide to Academic Research*. London: Kogan Page.

Bogdan, R.G. and Biklen, S. K. (1992) *Qualitative Research for Education* (2nd edition). Boston, MA: Allyn and Bacon.

Bolat, O. (2013) 'A non-positional teacher leadership approach to school improvement: an action research study in Turkey.' Unpublished PhD thesis, University of Cambridge, UK.

Borg, E. and Deane, M. (2011) Measuring the outcomes of individualised writing instruction: a multilayered approach to capturing changes in students' texts, *Teaching in Higher Education*, 16(3): 319–31.

Borg, W. and Gall, M. (1989) *Educational Research*. New York: Longman.

Bos, W. and Tarnai, C. (1999) Content analysis in empirical social research, *International Journal of Educational Research*, 31(8): 659–71.

Bowden, R., Bourner, T. and Laing, S. (2002) Professional doctorates in England and Australia: not a world of difference, *Higher Education Review*, 35(1): 2–23.

Brantlinger, A. (2011) Rethinking critical mathematics: a comparative analysis of critical, reform, and traditional geometry instructional texts, *Educational Studies in Mathematics*, 78(3): 395–411.

Briggs, A. and Coleman, M. (eds) (2007) *Research Methods in Educational Leadership and Management* (2nd edition). London: Sage.

Briggs, A., Coleman, M. and Morrison, M. (2012) *Research Methods in Educational Leadership* (3rd edition). London: Sage.

Brock-Utne, B. (1996) Reliability and validity in qualitative research within education in Africa, *International Review of Education*, 42(6): 605–21.

Brown, A. and Dowling, P. (1998) *Doing Research, Reading Research: A Mode of Interrogation for Education*. London: Falmer.

Brundrett, M. (ed.) (1999) *Principles of School Leadership*. King's Lynn: Peter Francis.

Brundrett, M. (2000) *Beyond Competence: The Challenge for Educational Management*. King's Lynn: Peter Francis.

Brundrett, M. (ed.) (2013) *Principles of School Leadership* (2nd edition). London: Sage.

Brundrett, M. and Burton, N. (2005) *Leading the Curriculum in the Primary School*. London: Sage.

Brundrett, M. and Crawford, M. (eds) (2008) *Developing School Leaders: An International Perspective*. London: Routledge.

Brundrett, M. and Rhodes, C. (2010) *Leadership for Learning: Quality and Accountability in Education*. London: Routledge.

Brundrett, M. and Terrell, I. (eds) (2004) *Learning to Lead in the Secondary School: Becoming an Effective Head of Department*. London: RoutledgeFalmer.

Bryman, A. (1988) *Quantity and Quality in Social Research*. London: Routledge.

Bryman, A. (2001) *Social Research Methods*. Oxford: Oxford University Press.

Bryman, A. (2004) *Social Research Methods* (2nd edition). Oxford: Oxford University Press.

Bryman, A. and Cramer, D. (1997) *Quantitative Data Analysis*. London: Routledge.

Burton, D. and Bartlett, S. (2005) *Practitioner Research for Teachers*. London: Sage.

Burton, N. and Brundrett, M. (2005) *Leading the Curriculum in the Primary School*. London: Sage.

Burton, N., Brundrett, M. and Jones, M. (2008) *Doing Your Education Research Project*. London: Sage.

Bush, T. (2007) 'Authenticity in research – reliability, validity and triangulation', in A. Briggs and M. Coleman (eds), *Research Methods in Educational Leadership and Management* (2nd edition). London: Sage.

Bush, T. (2008) *Leadership and Management Development in Education*. London: Sage.

Bush, T. (2009) Leadership development and school improvement: contemporary issues in leadership development, *Educational Review*, 61(4): 375–89.

Bush, T. (2010) 'Introduction: new directions in educational leadership', in T. Bush, L. Bell and D. Middlewood (eds), *The Principles of Educational Leadership and Management* (2nd edition). London: Sage. pp. 3–12.

Bush, T. (2010a) Editorial: The Significance of Leadership Theory, *Educational Management Administration and Leadership*, 38(3): 266–70.

Bush, T. (2011) *Theories of Educational Leadership and Management* (4th edition). London: Sage.

Campbell, A., McNamara, O. and Gilroy, P. (2004) *Practitioner Research and Professional Development in Education.* London: Paul Chapman.

Capobianco, B.M. and Feldman, A. (2006) Promoting quality for teacher action research: lessons learned from science teachers' action research, *Educational Action Research,* 14(4): 497–512.

Carr, W. and Kemmis, S. (1986) *Becoming Critical: Education, Knowledge and Action Research.* London: Falmer.

Chioncel, N.E., Van Der Veen, R.G.W., Wildemeersch, D. and Jarvis, P. (2003) The validity and reliability of focus groups as a research method in adult education, *International Journal of Lifelong Learning,* 22(5): 495–517.

Clegg, F. (1994) *Simple Statistics: A Course Book for the Social Sciences.* Cambridge: Cambridge University Press.

Coe, R. (2002) 'It's the Effect Size Stupid: What Effect Size is and Why it is Important'. Paper presented at the Annual Conference of the British Educational Research Association, University of Exeter, 12–14 September.

Cohen, L. and Holliday, M. (1996) *Practical Statistics for Students.* London: Paul Chapman.

Cohen, L., Manion, L. and Morrison, K. (2000) *Research Methods in Education.* London: RoutledgeFalmer.

Cohen, L., Manion, L. and Morrison, K. (2003) *Research Methods in Education* (5th edition). London: RoutledgeFalmer.

Cohen, L., Manion, L. and Morrison, K. (2007) *Research Methods in Education* (6th edition). Abingdon: Routledge.

Coleman, M. (2005) 'Evaluation in education', in M. Coleman and P. Earley (eds), *Leadership and Management in Education: Cultures, Change and Context.* Oxford, Oxford University Press. pp. 152–66.

Cook, T. (1998) The importance of mess in action research, *Educational Action Research Journal,* 6(1): 93–109.

Creemers, B.P.M., Kyriakides, L. and Sammons, P. (2010) *Methodological Advances in Educational Effectiveness Research (Quantitative Methodology Series).* London: Routledge.

Cziko, G. (1989) Unpredictability and indeterminism in human behaviour: arguments and implications for educational research, *Educational Researcher,* 18(3): 17–25.

Dadds, M. (1995) *Passionate Inquiry and School Development.* London: Falmer.

Dadds, M. and Hart, S. (2001) *Doing Practitioner Research Differently.* London: Routledge.

Davies, B. and Brundrett, M. (eds) (2010) *Developing Successful Leadership.* New York: Springer.

Davies, L. (1999) *Distance Education in Research Methodology: Ways of Doing Research: Unit One: Researching a Theory.* Birmingham: School of Education and Continuing Studies.

De Landsheere, G. (1993) 'History of educational research', in M. Hammersley (ed.), *Educational Research: Current Issues.,* London: The Open University and Paul Chapman Publishing. pp. 3–15.

Denscombe, M. (2003) *The Good Research Guide* (2nd edition). Maidenhead: Open University Press. (See Chapter 7 entitled 'Phenomenology', particularly the North American version: pp. 103–5.)

Denzin, N.K. (1970) *The Research Act in Sociology.* London: Butterworths.

Department for Education and Employment (DfEE) (2000) *Best Practice Research Scholarships: Guidance Notes for Teacher Applications.* London: DfEE.

Devers, K.J. and Frankel, R.M. (2000) Study design in qualitative research – 2: sampling and data collection strategies, *Education for Health*, 13(2): 263–71.

Dickens, L. and Watkins, K. (1999) Action research: rethinking Lewin, *Management Learning*, 30(2): 127–140.

Dowling, P. (1998) *The Sociology of Mathematics Education: Mathematical Myths/Pedagogic Texts*. London: Falmer.

Drever, E. (1995) *Using Semi-Structured Interviews in Small Scale Research*. Edinburgh: The SCRE Centre.

Ebbutt, D. (1985) 'Educational action research: some concerns and specific quibbles', in R. Burgess (ed.), *Issues in Educational Research*. Lewes: Falmer.

Edwards, A. and Talbot, R. (1994) *The Hard Pressed Researcher*. London: Longman.

Elliott, J. (1991) *Action Research for Educational Change*. Buckingham: Open University Press.

Elliott, J. (2005) Becoming critical: the failure to connect, *Educational Action Research*, 13(3): 221–34.

English, F. (2002) Cutting the Gordian knot of educational administration: the theory-practice gap, *The Review*, 44(1): 1–3.

EPPI Centre (2007a) *Reviews of research evidence are not necessarily rigorous or explicit in their methods of review*. Available at http://eppi.ioe.ac.uk/cms/Default.aspx?tabid=67 (last accessed 21 August 2007).

EPPI Centre (2007b) *Why is it important to be systematic?* Available at http://eppi.ioe.ac.uk/cms/Default.aspx?tabid=69 (last accessed 21 August 2007).

EPPI Centre (2007c) *Different types of review*. Available at http://eppi.ioe.ac.uk/cms/Default.aspx?tabid=1915 (last accessed on 21 August 2007).

EPPI Centre (2007d) *Administrative systems*. Available at http://eppi.ioe.ac.uk/cms/Default.aspx?tabid=1918 (last accessed on 21 August 2007).

EPPI Centre (2007e) *Synthesis*. Available at http://eppi.ioe.ac.uk/cms/Default.aspx?tabid=178 (last accessed on 21 August 2007).

Eraut, M. (1994) *Developing Professional Practice*. London: RoutledgeFalmer.

Feldman, A. (2007) Validity and quality in action research, *Educational Action Research*, 15(1): 21–32.

Field, A. (2009) *Discovering Statistics Using SPSS* (3rd edition). London: Sage.

Field, J. (2000) Researching lifelong learning through focus groups, *Journal of Further and Higher Education*, 24(3): 323–35.

Fogelman, K. and Comber, C. (2007) 'Surveys and sampling', in A. Briggs and M. Coleman (eds), *Research Methods in Educational Leadership and Management* (2nd edition). London: Sage.

Fowler, F.J. (1998) 'Design and evaluation of survey questions'. in L. Bickman and D. Rog (eds), *Handbook of Applied Social Research Methods*. London: Sage.

Foy, P. (1998) Sampling issues in international assessments, *International Journal of Educational Research*, 29(6): 555–68.

Fullan, M. (1993) *Change Forces: Probing the Depths of Educational Reform*. London: Falmer.

Fullan, M. (1999) *Change Forces: The Sequel*. London: Falmer.

Fullan, M. (2003) *Change Forces with a Vengeance*. London: RoutledgeFalmer.

Furlong, J. and Oancea, A. (2005) *Assessing Quality in Applied and Practice-Based Educational Research: A Framework for Discussion*. Oxford: Oxford University Department of Educational Studies.

Gall, M.D., Gall, J.P. and Borg, W.R. (2006) *Educational Research: An Introduction.* New York: Pearson.

Gardner, S.K. (2007) 'I heard it through the grapevine': doctoral student socialization in chemistry and history, *Higher Education,* 54: 723–40.

Gardner, S.K. (2009) Student and faculty attributions of attrition in high and low-completing doctoral programs in the United States, *Higher Education,* 58: 97–112.

Gatfield, T. (2005) An investigation into PhD supervisory management styles: development of a dynamic conceptual model and its managerial implications, *Journal of Higher Education Policy and Management,* 27(3): 311–25.

Gill, D. and Griffin, A. (2010) Good medical practice: what are we trying to say? Textual analysis using tag clouds, *Medical Education,* 44: 316–22.

Gillham, B. (2000) *Developing a Questionnaire* (2nd edition). London: Continuum.

Glaser, B. and Strauss, A. (1967) *The Discovery of Grounded Theory.* Chicago, IL: Aldine.

Goodman, J. and Grosvenor, I. (2009) Educational research – history of education: a curious case?, *Oxford Review of Education,* 35(5): 601–16.

Gorard, S. (2002) Political control: a way forward for educational research?, *British Journal of Educational Studies,* 50(3): 378–389.

Gorard, S. (2005) Current contexts for research in educational leadership and management, *Educational Management Administration and Leadership,* 33(2): 155–64.

Gorard, S. (2008) Research is easy, *University of Birmingham School of Education Research Student Newsletter, Spring,* pp.1–4.

Gorard, S. and See, B.H. (2011) How can we enhance enjoyment of secondary school? The student view, *British Educational Research Journal,* 37(4): 671–90.

Gough, D., Oliver, S. and Thomas, J. (2012) *An Introduction to Systematic Reviews.* London: Sage.

Gray, D.E. (2004) *Doing Research in the Real World.* London: Sage.

Greenway, C. (2011) 'The Influence of Ofsted in Early Years Education'. Unpublished PhD Thesis, University of Birmingham, UK.

Gronn, P. (2010) 'Where to next for educational leadership?', in T. Bush, L. Bell and D. Middlewood (eds), *The Principles of Educational Leadership and Management* (2nd edition). London: Sage. pp.70–86.

Gronn, P. and Ribbins, P. (1996) Leaders in context: postpositivist approaches to understanding educational leadership, *Educational Administration Quarterly,* 32(3): 452–73.

Grosvenor, I., Lawn, M., Novoa, A., Rousmaniere, K. and Smaller, H. (2004) Reading educational spaces: the photographs of Paulo Catrica, *Paedagogica Historica,* 40(3): 317–32.

Ground-Water Smith, S. and Mockler, N. (2007) *Facilitating Practitioner Research.* London: Routledge.

Gunter, H. and Ribbins, P. (2003) The field of educational leadership: studying maps and mapping studies, *British Journal of Educational Studies,* 51(3): 254–81.

Hallinger, P. and Snidvongs, K. (2005) *Adding Value to School Leadership and Management: A Review of Trends in the Development of Managers in the Education and Business Sectors.* Available at www.ncsl.org.uk/publications (last accessed 10 December 2009).

Hammersley, M. (1992) *What's Wrong With Ethnography?* London: Routledge.

Hammersley, M. (ed.) (1993a) *Social Research: Philosophy, Politics and Practice.* London: Open University Press.

Hammersley, M. (1993b) On the teacher as researcher, *Educational Action Research,* 1(3): 425–45.

Hammersley, M. (2008) Troubling criteria: a critical commentary on Furlong and Oancea's Framework for Assessing Educational Research, *British Educational Research Journal*, 34(6): 747–62.

Hargreaves, A. and Fink, D. (2006) *Sustainable Leadership*. San Francisco, CA: Jossey-Bass.

Harris, A. (2009) *Distributed Leadership: Different Perspectives*. Dordrecht: Springer.

Hart, C. (1998) *Doing a Literature Review: Releasing the Social Science Research Imagination*. London: Sage.

Hartley, D. (2007) The emergence of distributed leadership in education: why now? *British Journal of Educational Studies*, 55(2): 202–14.

Hartley, D. (2010) Paradigms: how far does research in distributed leadership 'stretch'?, *Educational Management Administration and Leadership*, 38(3): 271–85.

Heikkinen, H., Huttunen, R. and Syrjala, L. (2007) Action research as narrative: five principles for validation, *Educational Action Research*, 15(1): 5–19.

Herr, K. and Anderson, G.L. (2005) *The Action Research Dissertation: A Guide for Students and Faculty*. Thousand Oaks, CA: Sage.

Hockey, J. and Allen-Collinson, J. (2005) Identity change: doctoral students in art and design, *Arts and Humanities in Higher Education*, 4: 77–93.

Hopwood, N. (2010) Doctoral experience and learning from a sociocultural perspective, *Studies in Higher Education*, 35(7): 829–43.

Hoyle, E. (1980) 'Professionalisation and deprofessionalisation in education', in E. Hoyle and J. Megarry (eds), *World Yearbook of Education 1980: Professional Development of Teachers*. London: Kogan Page.

Jarvis, A. (2011) 'School Effectiveness and the Subject Leader's Influence Space: An Exploration of the Influence of Secondary School Subject leaders on the Professional practice of the members of their Departments'. Unpublished PhD Thesis, University of Birmingham, UK.

Johnson, L., Lee, A. and Green, B. (2000) The PhD and the autonomous self: gender, rationality and postgraduate pedagogy, *Studies in Higher Education*, 25(2): 135–147.

Johnson, R.B. and Onwuegbuzie, A.J. (2004) Mixed methods research: a research paradigm whose time has come, *Educational Researcher*, 33(7): 14–26.

Johnson, R.B., Onwuegbuzie, A.J. and Turner, L.A. (2007) Towards a definition of mixed methods research, *Journal of Mixed Methods Research*, 1(2): 112–33.

Joyce, B. (1991) The doors to school improvement, *Educational Leadership*, May: 59–62.

Joyce, B., Calhoun, E. and Hopkins, D. (1999) *The New Structure of School Improvement: Inquiring Schools and Achieving Students*. Buckingham: Open University Press.

Jung, J. (2012) The focus, role, and meaning of experienced teachers' reflection in physical education, *Physical Education and Sport Pedagogy*, 17(2): 157–75.

Kaplan, A. (1964) *The Conduct of Enquiry*. San Francisco, CA: Chandler.

Kemmis, S. (1980) 'Action research in retrospect and prospect', mimeo presented at the Annual General Meeting of the Australian Association for Research in Education, Sydney, November.

Kemmis, S. (2007) 'Action research', in M. Hammersley (ed.), *Educational Research and Evidence Based Practice*. Thousand Oaks, CA: Sage.

Kemmis, S. and McTaggart, R. (eds) (1992) *The Action Research Planner* (3rd edition). Victoria: Deakin University Press.

Kemmis, S. and McTaggart, R. (eds) (1997) *The Action Research Planner* (3rd edition). Victoria, Australia: Deakin University Press.

Keser, F., Akar, H. and Yildirim, A. (2011) The role of extracurricular activities in active citizenship education, *Journal of Curriculum Studies*, 43(6): 809–37.

Kirsz, A.S. (2007) 'A Case Study of the Knowledge and Understanding of Leadership Amongst Leaders in the Scout Association in an English City'. Unpublished EdD Thesis, University of Birmingham, UK.

Krathwohl, D.R. (1985) *Social and Behavioural Science Research*. San Francisco: Jossey-Bass.

Krueger, R.A. and Casey, M.A. (2000) *Focus Groups* (3rd edition). London: Sage.

Kuenssberg, S. (2011) The discourse of self-presentation in Scottish university mission statements, *Quality in Higher Education*, 17(3): 279–98.

Kvale, S. (1996) *Interviews*. London: Sage.

Kvale, S. (2007) *Doing Interviews*. London: Sage.

Labaree, D.F. (2003) The peculiar problems of preparing educational researchers, *Educational Researcher*, 32(4): 13–22.

Lambert, M. (2008) Devil in the detail: using pupil questionnaire survey in an evaluation of out-of-school classes for gifted and talented children, *Education 3–13*, 36(1): 69–78.

Lambert, M. (2012) *A Beginner's Guide to Doing Your First Education Research Project*. London: Sage.

Lee, A. (2008) How are doctoral students supervised? Concepts of doctoral research supervision, *Studies in Higher Education*, 33(3): 267–81.

Leithwood, K., Day, C., Sammons, P., Harris, A. and Hopkins, D. (2007) *Seven Strong Claims about Successful School Leadership*. London: Department for Education and Skills.

Lewin, K. (1946) Action research and minority problems, *Journal of Social Issues*, 2: 34–46.

Lewin, K. (1952) 'Group decision and social change', in G.W. Sweanson, T.M. Newcomb and E.L. Hartley (eds), *Readings in Social Psychology*. New York: Henry Holt & Co. (Reprinted in S. Kemmis and R. McTaggart, 1988, *The Action Research Reader,* 3rd edition. Geelong: Deakin University Press. pp. 47–56.)

Lincoln, Y. and Guba, E. (1985) *Naturalistic Enquiry*. Newbury Park, CA: Sage.

Lomax, P. (1990) 'An action research approach to developing staff in schools', in P. Lomax (ed.), *Managing Staff Development in Schools*. Clevedon: Multi-Lingual Matters. pp. 2–7.

Lumby, J. (2010) 'Leadership for diversity and inclusion', in T. Bush, L. Bell and D. Middlewood (eds), *The Principles of Educational leadership and Management* (2nd edition). London: Sage. pp. 219–35.

MacBeath, J (1999) *Schools Must Speak for Themselves*. London: Routledge.

MacBeath, J. and Dempster, N. (eds) (2009) *Connecting Leadership and Learning: Principles for Practice*. London: Routledge.

MacBeath, J., Schratz, M., Meuret, D. and Jakobsen, L. (2000) *Self-evaluation in European Schools: A Story of Change*. London: Routledge.

Mainhard, T., van der Rijst, R. and Wubbels, T. (2009) A model for the supervisor-doctoral student relationship, *Higher Education*, 58: 359–73.

Martinsuo, M. and Turkulainen, V. (2011) Personal commitment, support and progress in doctoral studies, *Studies in Higher Education*, 36(1): 103–20.

Maxwell, J.A. (1998) 'Designing a qualitative study', in L. Bickman and D. Rog (eds), *Handbook of Applied Social Research Methods*. London: Sage.

McKernan, J. (1991) *Curriculum Action Research*. London: Kogan Page.

McNiff, J., Lomax, P. and Whitehead, J. (1996) *You and Your Action Research Project*. London: Routledge.

Meyer, J.H.F. and Shanahan, M.P. (2004) Developing metalearning capacity in students: actionable theory and practical lessons learned in first-year economics, *Innovations in Education and Teaching International*, 41(4): 443–58.

Miles, M. and Huberman, A. (1994) *Qualitative Data Analysis*. Thousand Oaks, CA: Sage.

Mitchell, V. (1998) Improving mail survey responses from UK academics: some empirical findings, *Assessment and Evaluation in Higher Education*, 23(1): 59–70.

Morris, D. and Ecclesfield, N. (2011) A new computer-aided technique for qualitative document analysis, *International Journal of Research and Method in Education*, 34(3): 241–54.

Morrison, K. (1993) *Planning and Accomplishing School-Centred Evaluation*. Dereham: Peter Francis.

Morrison, K. (1998) *Management Theories for Educational Change*. London: Paul Chapman.

Morrison, M. (2002) 'What do we mean by educational research?', in M. Coleman and A. Briggs (eds), *Research Methods in Educational Leadership and Management*. London: Paul Chapman.

Muijs, D. (2006) New Directions for school effectiveness research: towards school effectiveness without schools, *Journal of Educational Change*, 7(3): 141–60.

Munn, P. and Drever, E. (1995) *Using Questionnaire in Small-Scale Research*. Edinburgh: The Scottish Council for Research in Education.

National College for School Leadership (NCSL) (2003) *Networked Learning Communities*. Nottingham: National College for School Leadership.

Newby, P. (2012) *Research Methods for Education*. London: Longman.

Norris, N. (1997) Error, bias and validity in qualitative research, *Educational Action Research*, 5(1): 172–176.

Pallant, J. (2010) *SPSS Survival Manual: A Step by Step Guide to Data Analysis Using SPSS*. Maidenhead: Open University Press.

Parlett, M. and Hamilton, D. (1972) Evaluation as illumination: a new approach to the study of inventory programmes. Reprinted in D. Hamilton (1977), *Beyond the Numbers Game*, London: Macmillan.

Pell, A. and Fogelman, K. (2007) 'Analysing quantitative data', in A. Briggs and M. Coleman (eds), *Research Methods in Educational Leadership and Management* (2nd edition). London: Sage.

Petersen, E.B. (2007) Negotiating academicity: postgraduate research supervision as category boundary work, *Studies in Higher Education*, 32(4): 475–87.

Pilkington, R.M. (2009) Practitioner research in education: the critical perspectives of doctoral students, *Studies in the Education of Adults*, 41(2): 154–174.

Plano Clark, V.L. and Cresswell, J.W. (2008) *The Mixed Methods Reader*. London: Sage.

PricewaterhouseCoopers (2007) *Independent Study into School Leadership* (RB818). Nottingham: DfES.

Rhodes, C.P. and Bisschoff, T. (2012) 'Leadership and school effectiveness', in J. Arthur and A. Peterson (eds), *The Routledge Companion to Education*. London: Routledge.

Rhodes, C.P. and Brundrett, M. (2010) 'Leadership for learning', in T. Bush, L. Bell and D. Middlewood (eds), *The Principles of Educational Leadership and Management* (2nd edition). London: Sage. pp. 153–75.

Rhodes, C.P., Hollinshead, A. and Nevill, A. (2007) Changing times, changing lives: a new look at job satisfaction in two university Schools of Education located in the English West Midlands, *Research in Post-Compulsory Education*, 12(1): 71–89.

Rhodes, C.P., Brundrett, M. and Nevill, A. (2008) Leadership talent identification and development, *Educational Management Administration and Leadership*, 36(3): 301–25.

Ribbins, P. and Gunter, H. (2002) Mapping leadership studies in education: towards a typology of knowledge domains, *Educational Management and Administration*, 30(4): 359–385.

Robson, C. (1993) *Real World Research*. Oxford: Blackwell.

Robson, C. (2002) *Real World Research* (2nd edition). Oxford: Blackwell.

Robson, C. (2006) *Real World Research* (3rd edition). Oxford: Blackwell.

Rost, J.C. (1991) *Leadership for the Twenty First Century*. Westport, CT: Praeger.

Salomon, G. (1991) Transcending the qualitative-quantitative debate: the analytic and systemic approaches to educational research, *Educational Researcher*, August – September: 10–18.

Sarantakos, S. (1998) *Social Research*. London: Palgrave Macmillan.

Schofield, J.W. (1989) 'Increasing the generalisability of qualitative research', in E.W. Eisner and A. Peshkin (eds), *Qualitative Inquiry in Education: The Continuation Debate*. New York: Teachers College Press.

Schön, D. (1983) *The Reflective Practitioner*. New York: Basic.

Scott, D. (1996) 'Methods and data in educational research', in D. Scott and R. Usher (eds), *Understanding Educational Research*. London: Routledge.

Scott, D. and Morrison, M. (2007) *Key Ideas in Educational Research*. London: Continuum.

Scott, D. and Morrison, M. (2010) New sites and agents for research education in the United Kingdom: making and taking doctoral identities, *Work Based Learning e-Journal*, 1(1): 15–34.

Scott, D., Brown, A., Lunt, I. and Thorne, L. (2004) *Professional Doctorates: Integrating Professional and Academic Knowledge*. Berkshire: The Open University Press.

Scott, J. (1990) *A Matter of Record: Documentary Sources in Social Research*. Cambridge: Polity.

Silverman, D. (1993) *Interpreting Qualitative Data*. London: Sage.

Silverman, D. (2004) *Qualitative Research: Theory, Method and Practice*. London: Sage.

Smith, P.K., Smith, C., Osborn, R. and Samara, M. (2008) A content analysis of school anti-bullying policies: progress and limitations, *Educational Psychology in Practice*, 24(1): 1–12.

Smith, S.C. and Bost, L.W. (2007) Collecting Post-School Outcome Data: Strategies for Increasing Response Rates, National Post-School Outcomes Center. Available at www.psocenter.org (last accessed July 2009).

Solomon, R. and Winch, C. (1994) *Calculating and Computing for the Social Science and Arts Students*. Buckingham: Open University Press.

Somekh, B. (1995) The contribution of action research to development in social endeavours: a position paper on action research methodology, *British Journal of Educational Research*, 21(3): 339–55.

Somekh, B. (2005) *Action Research: A Methodology for Change and Development*. London: Open University Press.

Southworth, G. (2002) 'Instructional leadership in schools: reflections and empirical evidence', *School Leadership and Management*, 22(1): 73–91.

Spillane, J. P. (2006) *Distributed Leadership*. San Francisco CA: Jossey-Bass.

Stake, R.E. (1995) *The Art of Case Study Research*. London: Sage.

Stenhouse, L. (1975) *An Introduction to Curriculum Research and Development*. London: Heinemann.

Strauss, A. and Corbin, J. (1990) *Basics of Qualitative Research: Grounded Theory Procedures and Techniques*. London: Sage.

Strauss, A. and Corbin, J. (1998) *Basics of Qualitative Research: Grounded Theory Procedures and Techniques* (2nd edition). London: Sage.

Symonds, J.E. and Gorard, S. (2010) Death of mixed methods? Or the rebirth of research as a craft, *Evaluation and Research in Education*, 23(2): 121–36.

Tashakkori, A. and Teddlie, A. (2010) *The SAGE Handbook of Mixed Methods in Social & Behavioral Research*. London: Sage.

Taylor, D. and Proctor, M. (2007) *The Literature Review: A Few Tips on Conducting It*. Toronto: University of Toronto. Available at www.utoronto.ca/writing/litrev.html (last accessed 21 August 2007).

Teddlie, C. and Reynolds, D. (eds) (2000) *The International Handbook of School Effectiveness Research*. London: Falmer.

Teddlie, C.B. and Tashakkori, A. (2008) *Foundations of Mixed Methods Research: Integrating Quantitative and Qualitative Approaches in the Social and Behavioral Sciences*. London: Sage.

Tesch, R. (1990) *Qualitative Research: Analysis Types and Software Tools*. New York: Falmer.

Thody, A. (2006) *Writing and Presenting Research*. London: Sage.

Thomas, A. (2007) Self-report data in cross-cultural research: issues of construct validity in questionnaires for quantitative research in educational leadership, *International Journal of Leadership in Education: Theory and Practice*, 10(2): 211–26.

Thomas, G. (1998) The myth of rational research, *British Educational Research Journal*, 24(2): 141–61.

Thomas, G. (2009) *How To Do Your Research Project*. London: Sage.

Thomas, G. and James, D. (2006) Reinventing grounded theory: some questions about theory, ground and discovery, *British Educational Research Journal*, 32(6): 767–95.

Torgerson, C.J. (2009) Randomised controlled trials in education research: a case study of an individually randomized pragmatic trial, *Education 3–13: International Journal of Primary, Elementary and Early Years Education*, 37(4): 313–21.

Trochim, W. (2002) *Positivism and Post-Positivism*. www.socialresearchmethods.net/kb/positvsm.htm (last accessed 18 July 2004).

Trochim, W. and Donnelly, J. (2006) *The Research Methods Knowledge Base* (3rd edition). Mason, OH: Atomic Dog.

Troyna, B. (1995) Beyond reasonable doubt? Researching 'race' in educational settings, *Oxford Review of Education*, 21(4): 155–65.

Tuckman, B. (1972) *Conducting Educational Research*. New York: Harcourt Brace Jovanovich.

University of Melbourne (2007a) *Conducting a Literature Review: Getting Started*. Available at www.lib.unimelb.edu.au/postgrad/litreview/gettingstarted.html (last accessed 21 August 2007).

University of Melbourne (2007b) *Conducting a Literature Review: Tips on Critical Reading*. Available at www.lib.unimelb.edu.au/postgrad/litreview/criticalreading.html (last accessed 21 August 2007).

Vanstone, M. and Kinsella, E. A. (2010) Critical reflection and prenatal screening public education materials: a metaphoric textual analysis, *Reflective Practice*, 11(4): 451–67.

Verma, G. and Mallick, K. (1999) *Researching Education: Perspectives and Techniques*. London: Falmer.

Walford, G. (2001) *Doing Qualitative Research: A Personal Guide to the Research Process*. London: Continuum.

Wallace, M. (2002) Modelling distributed leadership and management effectiveness: primary school senior management teams in England and Wales, *School Effectiveness and School Improvement*, 13(2): 163–86.

Wallace, M. and Poulson, L. (eds) (2003) *Learning to Read Critically in Educational Leadership and Management*. London: Sage.

Walliman, N. (2005) *Your Research Project.* London: Sage.

Waterson, J. (2000) Balancing research and action: reflections on an action research project in a social services department, *Social Policy Administration,* 34(4): 494–508.

Wilson, R. and Dewaele, J. (2010) The use of web questionnaires in second language acquisition and bilingualism research, *Second Language Research,* 26(1): 103–23.

Winograd, K. (2011) Sports biographies of African American football players: the racism of colour-blindness in children's literature, *Race Ethnicity and Education,* 14(3): 331–49.

Winter, R. (1998) Finding a voice, thinking with others: a conception of action research, *Educational Action Research,* 6: 53–68.

Winter, R. and Munn-Giddings, C. (2001) *A Handbook for Action Research in Health and Social Care.* London: Routledge.

Wisker, G., Morris, C., Cheng, M., Masika, R., Warnes, M., Trafford, V., Robinson, G. and Lilly, J. (2010) *Doctoral Learning Journeys Final Report,* Higher Education Academy, 1–61.

Wolcott, H.F. (1994) *Transforming Qualitative Data: Description, Analysis and Interpretation.* Thousand Oaks, CA: Sage.

Wragg, E.D. (1999) *An Introduction to Classroom Observation.* London: Routledge.

Wrigley, T. (2008) School improvement in a neo-liberal world, *Journal of Educational Administration and History,* 40(2): 129–48.

Yin, R.K. (1989) 'Designing single and multiple case studies', *Case Study Research: Design and Methods* (revised edition). London: Sage.

Youngman, M.B. (1994) Designing and Using Questionnaires, Rediguide 12, *Guides in Educational Research.* Nottingham: Rediguides.

Zhao, C.M., Golde, C.M. and McCormick, A.C. (2007) More than a signature: how advisor choice and advisor behaviour affect doctoral student satisfaction, *Journal of Further and Higher Education,* 31(3): 263–81.

Zuber-Skerritt, O. (ed.) (1996) *New Directions in Action Research.* London: Falmer.

Index